LINGUA 21

ENGLISH

you know...

W0284944

A2

REFERENCE BOOK

école-club
klubschule
scuola club
migros

Hueber

English A2

Reference book by Uta Trevor
The vocabulary was adapted by Keith Sprague and Lee Walker

This adaptation is based on *English Elements 2* and *English Elements 3* by:
Myriam Fischer Callus
Annie Roth
Jackie Sykes

Club Schools Migros
Lingua 21 project co-ordinator: Mike Makosch
Project manager for English: Gareth Hughes
Specifications group: Gabriela Graf, Yvonne de Henseler, Oonagh Heron, Lee Walker
Consultative group: Jennifer Audenis, Celeste Berger, Estelle Bieri, Claudia Canta, Joy Fournier, Jayne Herzog, Charlotte Lehmann, Helga Plank, Danielle Rappan, Catherine Schrago
Editorial assistant: Martina Wernli

Max Hueber Publishers
Lingua 21 project co-ordinator: Veronika Kirschstein
Project manager: Rebecka Howe
Production manager: Doris Hagen
Illustrations: Sina Scheller-Persenico
Printed and bound by: Ludwig Auer GmbH, Donauwörth

3.	2.	1.		
2007	06	05	04	03

First published 2003

Printed in Germany
ISBN 3-19-318502-7

1. Verbs .... page 6

1.1 To be .... page 6
1.1.1 Present simple .... page 6
1.1.2 Past simple .... page 7
1.1.3 There is / there are .... page 8

1.2 To have .... page 9
1.2.1 Present simple .... page 9
1.2.2 Past simple .... page 12

1.3 Present tenses .... page 13
1.3.1 Present simple .... page 13
1.3.2 Present continuous .... page 14

1.4 Past tenses .... page 16
1.4.1 Past simple .... page 16
1.4.2 Past continuous .... page 19
1.4.3 Used to .... page 21

1.5 Present perfect .... page 22

1.6 Future .... page 24
1.6.1 Will .... page 24
1.6.2 Present continuous .... page 26
1.6.3 Going to .... page 27

1.7 Modal verbs .... page 29

1.8 Passive .... page 32

1.9 Conditional .... page 32

1.10 Imperatives .... page 33

2. Nouns, pronouns and determiners .... page 34

2.1 Nouns .... page 34
2.1.1 Plurals .... page 35
2.1.2 Countable and uncountable nouns .... page 36

2.2 Articles .... page 38
2.2.1 Indefinite article .... page 38
2.2.2 Definite article .... page 39

2.3 This/that, these/those .... page 39

2.4 Pronouns .... page 40
2.4.1 Subject and object pronouns .... page 40
2.4.2 Indefinite pronouns .... page 41
2.4.3 Relative pronouns .... page 42

2.5 Possessives .... page 43
2.5.1 Possessive determiners / adjectives .... page 43
2.5.2 's / of .... page 44

2.6 Quantifiers .... page 44
2.6.1 Some / any / no .... page 44
2.6.2 Much / many / a lot of .... page 45
2.6.3 Both / all .... page 46
2.6.4 Each / every .... page 47

3. Adjectives .... page 47

3.1 Comparison of adjectives .... page 48
3.1.1 Comparative and superlative form .... page 48

4. Adverbs .... page 50
4.1 Adverbs of frequency .... page 50
4.2 Adverbs of manner .... page 51

5. Prepositions .... page 53
5.1 Prepositions of time .... page 53
5.2 Prepositions of place and movement .... page 54

6. Sentences .... page 56

6.1 Question words .... page 56
6.1.1 When / where / why .... page 56
6.1.2 How .... page 57
6.1.3 Who / what .... page 57
6.1.4 Which / what .... page 57

7. Appendix .... page 58

7.1 List of irregular verbs .... page 58

7.2 Verb patterns .... page 59

7.3 Numbers .... page 62

7.4 Ordinal numbers .... page 62

7.5 Telling the time .... page 62

8. Communication .... page 63

8.1 Giving directions .... page 63

8.2 Social situations .... page 64

8.3 Telephoning .... page 64

9. Vocabulary – unit by unit .... page 65

10. Index .... page 119

Hinweis: → Unit 2 verweist auf die Einheit im Coursebook A2.

Siehe 1.4.2: verweist auf das Kapitel im Referenzbuch.

1. Verbs (Verben)

1.1 To be

1.1.1 Present simple

Aussage und Verneinung

I'm from Switzerland.
He isn't from Britain.
Fiona is a teacher.
Thomas and Connie are students.

I	'm am	French.
He She It	's is	here.
We You They	're are	hungry.

I	'm not am not	French.
He She / It It	isn't 's not is not	here.
We / You / They You They	aren't 're not are not	hungry.

Frage und Kurzantwort

Is it eight o'clock? – Yes, it is.
Is she German? – No, she isn't.

Am	I	late?
Is	he she it	here?
Are	we you they	hungry?

Yes,	I	am.
	he she it	is.
	we you they	are.

No,	I	'm not. am not.
	he she it	isn't. 's not. is not.
	we you they	aren't. 're not. are not.

1.1.2 Past simple

Aussage und Verneinung

He was at the cinema last night.
We were in the airport for 15 hours.
It wasn't the same place.
Everything was different.

I He She It	was	fine.
We You They	were	

I He She It	wasn't was not	fine.
We You They	weren't were not	

Frage und Kurzantwort

Were you OK? – Yes, I was.
Were all the hotels full? – Yes, they were.
Was she happy? – Yes, she was.

Was	I he she it	there?
Were	we you they	

Yes,	I he she it	was.
	we you they	were.

No,	I he she it	wasn't. was not.
	we you they	weren't. were not.

→ Unit 4 1.1.3 There is / there are

There's a nice park next to the hotel.
There are 12 people in my English class.

There are a lot of people but there is no electricity.

> **Note**
> Der Ausdruck entspricht etwa dem deutschen „es gibt“ bzw. dem in der Schweiz gebräuchlichen „es hat/es sind“.

	Einzahl	Mehrzahl
Aussage	There is ... There's ...	There are ... There're ...
Verneinung	There isn't ...	There aren't ...
Frage	Is there ...?	Are there ...?
Kurzantwort	Yes, there is. No, there isn't.	Yes, there are. No, there aren't.

„There“ kann auch mit anderen Formen des Verbs „be“ kombiniert werden:

There was a storm last night.
There used to be an old house but now there is a supermarket.
There has been an accident.
There will be a big party at New Year's.
There could be a storm tonight.

Siehe 1.4.3

1.2 To have

1.2.1 Present simple

Have you got ...?

> ***Note***
>
> Im britischen Englisch wird eher „have got“ verwendet, während im amerikanischen Englisch „have“ üblicher ist. „Have got“ wird normalerweise nur im „present simple“ verwendet und in Grossbritannien gewöhnlich auch nur mündlich gebraucht und nicht geschrieben.

Aussage und Verneinung

I've got a brother, but I haven't got a sister.
He's got a bike, but he hasn't got a car.

I You We They	've got have got	a cold. a meeting. an Italian car. a nice name.
He She It	's got has got	

I You We They	haven't got	a cold. a meeting. an Italian car. a nice name.
He She It	hasn't got	

Frage und Kurzantwort

Have you got a brother? – No, I haven't
Has Fiona got a cold? – No, she hasn't.

Have	I you we they	got	a cold? a meeting? a nice name? an Italian car?
Has	he she it		

Yes,	I you we they	have.
	he she it	has.

No,	I you we they	haven't.
	he she it	hasn't.

Note

He's tired. = He **is** tired.
= Er ist müde.
He's got a car. = He **has** got a car.
= Er hat ein Auto.

Do you have ...?

Aussage und Verneinung

I have a brother, but I don't have a sister.
He has a bike, but he doesn't have a car.

I You We They	've have	a cold. a meeting. nice name. an Italian car.
He She It	's has	

I You We They	don't have do not have	a cold. a meeting. a nice name. an Italian car.
He She It	doesn't have does not have	

Frage und Kurzantwort

Do you have a sister? – No, I don't.
Does Fiona have a cold? – No, she doesn't.

Do	I you we they	have	a cold? a meeting? a bed? an Italian car?
Does	he she it		

Yes,	I you we they	do.
	he she it	does.

No,	I you we they	don't.
	he she it	doesn't.

1.2.2 Past simple

Aussage

I You We They He She It	had	a cold. a meeting. a bed. an Italian car.

Verneinung und Frage

Beide Formen werden mit „did" (Vergangenheitsform von „do") gebildet.

I You We They He She It	didn't did not	have	a cold. a meeting. a nice name. an Italian car.

Did	I you we they he she it	have	a cold? a meeting? a nice name? an Italian car?

1.3 Present tenses (Gegenwartsformen)

→ Unit 1

1.3.1 Present simple

I come from Austria.	*(Wohnort)*
She likes Mozart.	*(Vorlieben und Abneigungen)*
I always have breakfast before I leave the house.	*(Alltag)*
Antonio works in an office.	*(Arbeit)*
I go swimming twice a week.	*(regelmässige Abmachungen)*
The train leaves at 7.46.	*(Fahrplanzeiten)*

Das „present simple" wird verwendet, um Tatsachen oder Gewohnheiten zu beschreiben, die für die Gegenwart, die Vergangenheit und die Zukunft gültig sind. Es ist quasi eine zeitlose Form.

> *Note*
>
> **Signalwörter**
> - always, sometimes, often, usually, never
> - every day, every Tuesday

Aussage und Verneinung

I You We They	start	at 9 o'clock.
He She It	starts	

I You We They	don't do not	start	at 9 o'clock.
He She It	doesn't does not		

> ### Note
> In der Verneinung wird das „s“ dem Hilfsverb „do“ angehängt, nicht dem Hauptverb.
>
> *„She doesn't work.“* nicht: *„~~She doesn't works.~~“*

Frage

Do	I you we they	start	at 9 o'clock?
Does	he she it		

Kurzanwort

Yes,	I you we they	do.
	he she it	does.

No,	I you we they	don't. do not.
	he she it	doesn't. does not.

→ Unit 1, 2

1.3.2 Present continuous

“Hello is that you darling? I'm sitting on the train. Oops! We're just going through a tunnel …” (aktuelle Handlung)

– *“What are you doing in school this semester?”*
– *“I'm learning Spanish.”* (Tatsache, zeitlich begrenzt)

Das „present continuous“ wird gebraucht, um aktuelle Handlungen auszudrücken oder Tatsachen zu beschreiben, die für einen bestimmten Zeitraum gültig sind. Auf Deutsch existiert diese Form nicht. Sie kann in etwa übersetzt werden mit: „Ich bin gerade dabei, …“ (Im Dialekt sagt man: „Ich bin grad am …“). Das „present continuous“ wird auch Verlaufsform genannt. Siehe 1.6.2

Aussage und Verneinung

Die Form wird gebildet mit „to be“ und der Grundform des Verbs + Endung „-ing“.

I	’m am	going. cooking.
He She It	’s is	
We You They	’re are	

I	’m not am not	going. cooking.
He She It	isn’t ’s not is not	
We You They	aren’t ’re not are not	

Frage und Kurzantwort

Am	I	going? cooking?
Is	he she it	
Are	we you they	

Yes,	I	am.
	he she it	is.
	we you they	are.

No,	I	’m not. am not.
	he she it	isn’t. ’s not. is not.
	we you they	aren’t. are not.

> ### Note
> Wenn das Verb mit einem einzelnen Konsonanten endet (z.B. p), dem ein einzelner Vokal vorausgeht (z.B. o), wird der Konsonant verdoppelt.
> swi**m** → swi**mm**ing
> sto**p** → sto**pp**ing

Siehe 1.4.2

Das Schluss **-e** wird beim Anhängen von **-ing** weggelassen:

mov**e** → moving
com**e** → coming
mak**e** → making

1.4 Past tenses (Vergangenheitsformen)

→ Unit 2, 6

1.4.1 Past simple

The pilgrims celebrated the first Thanksgiving in 1621.
Connie played tennis last week.
Where did you live when you were a child?

> ### Note
> **Signalwörter**
> – yesterday, last week, last month, last year, in 1987, ...
>
> und das **Fragewort**:
> – When ...?

Im „past simple" gibt es regelmässige („regular") und unregelmässige („irregular") Verben.

Charlie Chaplin went to the USA in 1910.

Regelmässige Verben

Bei den regelmässigen Verben wird das „past simple" durch Anhängen von „-d" bzw. „-ed" gebildet.

*She live**d** in Lugano. She didn't live in Locarno.*
*He work**ed** in Olten. He didn't work in Aarau.*

Aussage

I You He She It We They	lived worked	here.

Verneinung

I You He She It We They	didn't did not	live work	here.

Note

Die Verneinung ist ersichtlich in „didn't", nicht im Verb.

She live**d** here.
She **didn't** live here.

Frage

Did	I you he she it we they	start?

Kurzantwort

Yes,	I you he she it we they	did.

No,	I you he she it we they	didn't / did not.

Spelling and pronunciation (**Schreibweise und Aussprache**)

Bei den regelmässigen Verben wird das „past simple“ durch Anhängen von „-d“ bzw. „-ed“ gebildet. Beachten Sie die unterschiedliche Schreibweise und Aussprache in folgenden Beispielen.

Endung **-e**	mov**e**	move**d**	**+ d**
Endung: Konsonant + **y**	marr**y**	marri**ed**	**y → i + ed**
aber: Vokal + **y**	sta**y**	sta**yed**	**y → y + ed**
Verben, die auf einen einzelnen Konsonanten enden, dem ein einzelner Vokal vorausgeht	sto**p**	sto**pped**	Verdoppelung der Konsonanten **+ ed**

Die Endung „-ed“ wird meist als [d] ausgesprochen, ausser wenn folgende Laute vorangehen:

nach	Aussprache als	Beispiel
ch, **f**, **gh**, **k**, **p**, **sh**, **s** oder **x**	[t]	[wɒtʃt], [la:ft], [kʊkt]
d oder **t**	[ɪd]	[endɪd], [sta:tɪd], [wɒntɪd]

Unregelmässige Verben

Viele der häufigsten Verben sind unregelmässig (irregular). Als unregelmässig werden diejenigen Verben bezeichnet, die das „past simple“ nicht durch Anhängen von „-ed“ bilden. Ihre Formen müssen auswendig gelernt werden. Ihre Form ist jedoch für alle Personen gleich. Im Anhang dieses Buches (7.1, Seite 58-59) gibt es eine Liste der wichtigsten Verben, die im Lehrbuch English A2 erscheinen.

1.4.2 Past continuous

→ Unit 13

Wie in der Gegenwart (present) gibt es im Englischen in der Vergangenheit (past) auch eine Verlaufsform (continuous). Auf Deutsch kennen wir diese Form nicht; man kann dies in etwa umschreiben mit: „Ich war gerade dabei, …“

While he was walking down the street he met his friend.

I	**was**	working.
he, she, it	**was**	
we, you, they	**were**	

Siehe 1.3.2

WALTERLI'S KNEES WERE SHAKING WHEN HIS FATHER SHOT THE ARROW.

Wir benutzen das „past continuous“, wenn …

– zwei Handlungen gleichzeitig, parallel zueinander abliefen.	*While I was having breakfast, I was thinking about my day's work.*
– eine länger andauernde Handlung im Hintergrund beschrieben wird. (Die kürzere, neu eingetretene Handlung wird im „past simple“ beschrieben).	*Barbara was taking Ammu to the hospital when the car broke down.* *We were watching TV when all the lights went out.*
– Hintergrundinformationen zu einer Geschichte gegeben werden.	*It was nearly midnight and he was lying on his bed, a torch in one hand and a book in the other …*

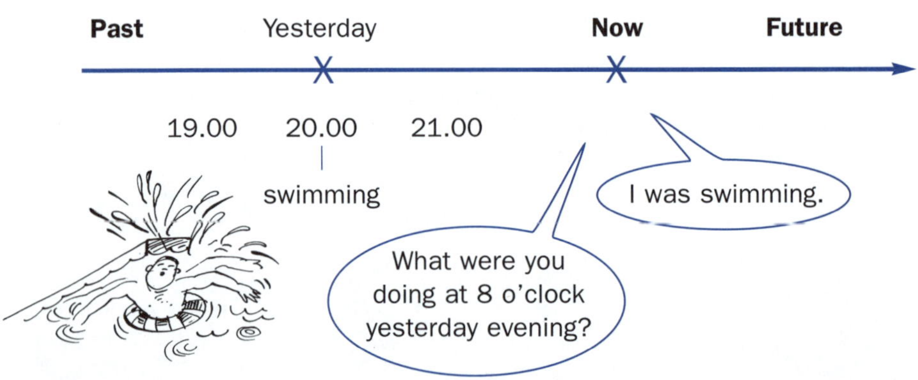

1.4.3 Used to

→ Unit 9,14

She used to speak Japanese quite well but she has forgotten most of it now.
There used to be many small shops in the village but now there is only one.

Anstelle des „past simple“ kann „used to“ benutzt werden, um von früheren Gewohnheiten zu sprechen, von lange andauernden Zuständen, die jetzt nicht mehr zutreffen.

Aussage

I, you, we he, she, it	used to	live in Fribourg. play football for the village team. smoke.

Verneinung

I, you, we he, she, it	didn't did not	use to	live in Fribourg. play football for the village team. smoke.

Frage

Did	I, you, we he, she, it	use to	live in Fribourg? play football for the village team? smoke?

Kurzantwort

Yes,	I, you, we	did.
No,	he, she, it	didn't. did not.

→ Unit 6, 8, 12, 14

1.5 Present perfect

Man benutzt das „present perfect“ um
– einen Zustand zu beschreiben, der in der Vergangenheit begonnen hat, aber noch nicht abgeschlossen wurde. Zum Beispiel:

Fiona has lived in Switzerland for five months / since January.
(Das heisst: Sie wohnt noch hier.)

– etwas in der Vergangenheit zu beschreiben, dessen genauer Zeitpunkt entweder unbekannt oder (im Moment) unwichtig ist. Zum Beispiel:

Have you ever travelled in a helicopter?
Fiona hasn't ever played roulette.

Note

Signalwörter

– already,
– ever
– for
– just
– lately
– never
– since
– so far
– yet

He's been a member of the club for over 50 years.

→ Unit 8, 14

„Since“ or „for“?

Für das deutsche Wort „seit“ gibt es auf Englisch zwei Präpositionen, die mit bestimmten Zeitausdrücken kombiniert werden.

since fixer Zeitpunkt	**for** Zeitdauer/ Zeitspanne
yesterday last Saturday my birthday 1998 I saw you	a week a whole month a year 10 years

Note

Auf Deutsch sagen wir: (Präsens) *Ich kenne ihn seit 10 Jahren.*
Auf Englisch sagen wir: (present perfect) *I've known him for 10 years.*

Das „present perfect" wird gebildet mit „have" und dem „past participle". Das „past participle" der regelmässigen Verben hat die gleiche Form wie das „past simple". Für die unregelmässigen Verben siehe 7.1, Seite 58-59.

Aussage

I You We They	've have	been to London. ridden a camel.
He She It	's has	

Verneinung

I You We They	haven't have not	been to London. ridden a camel.
He She It	hasn't has not	

Frage

Have	I you we they	been to London? started? made a mistake?
Has	he she it	

Kurzantwort

Yes,	I you we they	have.
	he she it	has.

No,	I you we they	haven't. have not.
	he she it	hasn't. has not.

> *Note*
>
> Im Gegensatz zum Deutschen oder Französischen wird das „present perfect" immer mit „have" gebildet.
>
> We have come. nicht: ~~We are come.~~
> I've just arrived. nicht: ~~I'm just arrived.~~

→ Unit 11

1.6 Future (Zukunftsformen)

1.6.1 Will (Siehe auch 1.7)

Man benutzt „will" für die Zukunft, wenn man spontan entscheidet, etwas zu tun:
– *I want to go out tonight. I'll ring Suzette and ask her if she's free.*
oder wenn man über Möglichkeiten in der Zukunft spricht:
– *I think I'll learn Chinese next year.*

Diese Form wird auch benutzt
um Vorhersagen zu machen:
– *You will meet a rich man.*
– *I think it'll rain this afternoon.*

Aussage

I You He She It We They	'll will	start tomorrow.

Verneinung

I You He She It We They	won't will not	start tomorrow.

Frage

Will	I you he she it we they	start tomorrow?

Kurzantwort

Yes,	I you he she it we they	will.

No,	I you he she it we they	won't. will not.

→ Unit 12 1.6.2 Present continuous

When are you leaving?
What are you doing this evening?
We're going to a concert at 8 o'clock.
Sarah is not working on Saturday.
David is doing a French course in the summer holidays.

Das „present continuous" kann verwendet werden, um über bereits getroffene Abmachungen für die Zukunft zu sprechen.

- *I'm doing a French course in the summer holidays.*
  (Der Kurs ist schon gebucht.)
- *He's doing a presentation at the weekend.*
  (Das Datum ist schon mit der Firma abgemacht.)
- *We're going to Italy in the holidays.*
  (Wir haben schon gebucht.)

Siehe 1.3.2

> ***Note***
>
> **Signalwörter**
> Das „present continuous" mit Zeitangaben wie den folgenden bezieht sich auf eine Abmachung für die Zukunft:
> - at/on the weekend
> - on Friday
> - in the summer holidays
> - tonight

→ Unit 5, 1

1.6.3 Going to

We're going to have a party.
I'm going to buy a computer.
We're going to do a computer course.

Wenn man über persönliche Absichten und Pläne spricht, aber noch keine festen Abmachungen getroffen hat, verwendet man die „going to“-Form.

Look at the black sky! It's going to rain!
She is going to have a baby.

Bei Vorhersagen, die auf aktuellen Zuständen basieren, benutzt man ebenfalls die „going-to“-Form.

Aussage und Verneinung

I	'm am	going to	walk to the station. buy a computer. have a baby.
He She It	's is		
We You They	are 're		

I	'm not am not	going to	walk to the station. have a baby.
He She It	isn't 's not is not		
We You They	aren't 're not		

Frage und Kurzantwort

Am	I	going to	walk to the station? buy a computer? have a baby?
Is	he she it		
Are	you we they		

Yes,	I	am.
	he she it	is.
	we you they	are.

No,	I	'm not. am not.
	he she it	's not. isn't. is not.
	we you they	aren't. 're not. are not.

Note

Der Unterschied zwischen festem Plan und persönlicher Absicht ist nicht immer klar ersichtlich. Deshalb kann oft sowohl das „present continuous" als auch „going to" eingesetzt werden.

We're going to have a party next Saturday.
We're having a party next Saturday.

1.7 Modal verbs (Modalverben)

I can't stay.
Could you help me, please?
I will send him an e-mail.
Would you like a cup of tea?
May I smoke?

Modalverben (modal verbs) haben folgende Eigenschaften:

- Sie werden zusammen mit der Grundform eines Verbs, aber ohne „to" verwendet.
- In der dritten Person wird kein „s" angefügt:
  It will rain. nicht: ~~*It wills rain.*~~
- Frageform und Verneinung werden wie folgt gebildet:

Aussage und Verneinung	She	will will not	come.
Frage	Will	she	come?

Aussage

I You He She It We They	can / could will / would may should	stay. help. go.

Verneinung

I You He She It We They	can't / couldn't cannot / could not won't / wouldn't will not / would not may not shouldn't / should not	stay. help. go.

Frage

Can Could Will Would May	I you he she it we they	stay? help? go?

Kurzantwort

Yes,	I you he she it we they	can. could. will. would. may.

No,	I you he she it we they	can't. couldn't. cannot. could not. won't. wouldn't. will not. would not. may not.

Hier eine Übersicht über die wichtigsten Modalverben und ihre Bedeutung.

→ Unit 1

can	*I can speak English.* *He can sing well.* *Can you swim?*	**Möglichkeit, Fähigkeit**
can could may	*Can I use your phone?* *Could I go home early?* *May I smoke here?*	**Erlaubnis, Bitte**
could, can	*Could you please give me a lift?* *Can you tell me the way?*	**um etwas bitten**
would	*Would you like a cup of tea?*	**Einladung**

should	*You should try to get more exercise.* *You shouldn't eat so much chocolate.*	**Rat, Ermahnung, Pflicht**	→ Unit 10
must have to need to mustn't	*In your new job you must be on time.* *I had to get up early this morning.* *Do I really have to go to school tomorrow, Mummy?* *You need to speak English with her.* *You mustn't smoke here.*	**äusserer Zwang** **Verpflichtung** **Notwendigkeit** **Verbot**	→ Unit 9, 10
needn't don't have to	*You needn't stay to the end if you are tired.* *You don't have to come, but it would be nice if you did.*	**etwas ist nicht notwendig**	→ Unit 13
will Siehe 1.6.1	*I'll be home at 6 o'clock.* *It'll probably rain tomorrow.*	**Futur**	

Note

False friends (falsche Freunde)

„will" (Deutsch) ≠ „will" (Englisch)
Ich **will** einen Kuchen backen. = I **want** to bake a cake.
Sie **werden** zum Mond fliegen. = You **will** fly to the moon.

mustn't ≠ muss nicht
Du darfst das nicht tun! = You **mustn't** do this!
Du musst das nicht tun, aber du darfst. = You **don't have to/needn't** do this, but you may.

→ Unit 7
1.8 Passive

Where is this chocolate made? – It's made in Switzerland.
When was this house built? – It was built in 1848.

Das Passiv wird verwendet, wenn bei einer Handlung das Objekt und nicht der Täter im Vordergrund steht. Passivformen werden oftmals in Sachtexten verwendet.

Es wird gebildet mit „to be“ + „past participle“. Siehe 7.1

Present	This chocolate **is** made in Switzerland.
Past	This house **was** built in 1848.

Für Fragen und Verneinung des Verbs „to be“, siehe 1.1

This picture was painted by Leonardo's son.

→ Unit 11
1.9 Conditional

if + present simple	**present simple**	**Type zero**
If you don't save data regularly, If I drink coffee in the evening,	you risk losing it. I don't sleep well.	Für allgemeingültige Situationen benutzen wir „present simple“ in beiden Satzteilen.
if + present simple	**will + infinitive**	**Type 1**
If the train is late, If you want to catch the train,	I'll call you. you'll have to hurry.	Wenn wir über etwas in der Zukunft sprechen, das passieren kann, benutzen wir „if“ und „will“.

> ### *Note*
>
> Die Reihenfolge der Sätze kann auch umgedreht werden, wobei dann kein Komma geschrieben wird.
>
> *I'll ring the office if I'm late.*
> *I risk losing the data if I don't save it regularly.*

1.10 Imperatives

➜ Unit 3

Sit down!
Let's go!
Try to get up 10 minutes earlier each day.
Please don't smoke.
Don't do too much too soon.

Die Befehlsform (imperative) wird im Englischen mit der Grundform (infinitive) ohne „to" gebildet. Man braucht sie, um Befehle zu erteilen und Ratschläge zu geben. Beachten Sie auch die „let's"-Form, z.B.: „Let's go!" (Gehen wir!).

Forms

	Positive	Negative
you	Stand up! Be quiet!	Don't stand up! Don't be noisy!
we	Let's go! Let's be sensible!	Let's not go! Let's not be silly!

2. Nouns, pronouns and determiners (Nomen, Pronomen und Begleiter)

Der Ausdruck „determiner“ wird in englischen Grammatiken für eine Anzahl Wörter benutzt, die vor einem „noun“ (Nomen oder auch Substantiv genannt) stehen.
„Determiner“ ist ein Sammelbegriff für verschiedene Wörter. Näheres zu den einzelnen Wörtern finden Sie in den folgenden Abschnitten.

determiner	**noun**	**see**
a	cat	indefinite article 2.2.1
the	cat	definite article 2.2.2
this	cat	demonstrative adjectives 2.3
my	cat	possessive adjectives 2.5
some	money	quantifiers 2.6
which	cat	question words 6.

2.1 Nouns (Nomen)

Ein Nomen (noun) ist eigentlich ein Name für eine Person oder eine Sache. Diese kann zum Anfassen sein, wie z.B. „chair“, „water“ oder abstrakt wie „idea“, „love“.
Andere Ausdrücke für Nomen sind Substantiv, Dingwort, Namenswort und Hauptwort.
Nur Eigennamen wie „Fiona“, „London“, „Switzerland“ werden im Englischen gross geschrieben.

→ Unit 3

2.1.1 Plurals (Mehrzahl)

Einzahl	Mehrzahl	Regel
hat / jumper / blouse	hats / jumpers / blouses	Die meisten Substantive bilden den Plural durch Anhängen von -s.
gla**ss** / wi**sh** / wat**ch** / bo**x** / bu**s**	glasses / wishes / watches / boxes / buses	Bei Substantiven, die auf einen Zischlaut (ch, s, sh oder x) enden, wird -es angehängt.
diar**y** / stor**y**	diaries / stories	Substantive mit Endung auf Konsonant + y ersetzen das y durch -ies.
b**oy** / d**ay**	boys / days	Substantive mit Endung auf Vokal + y nehmen die Endung -s.
child / woman / man / person	children / women / men / people	Nur wenige Substantive haben eine unregelmässige Mehrzahlform (irregular plural).
potat**o** tomat**o** pian**o** phot**o**	potatoes tomatoes pianos photos	Einige Substantive mit Endung auf -o hängen ein -es an. **Achtung:** Nicht alle Wörter, die auf -o enden, hängen ein -es an. Am besten schlagen Sie Wörter auf -o im Wörterbuch nach.

Unregelmässige Pluralbildung

child – children
man – men
woman – women
wife – wives
shelf – shelves
foot – feet
tooth – teeth

cats

→ Unit 3

2.1.2 Countable and uncountable nouns

Countable nouns		**Uncountable nouns**
Singular a banana an apple this cat	**Plural** three bananas many apples those cats	 (some) water (much) gold (some) love
„Countable nouns“ sind Substantive, die gezählt werden können. Sie haben eine Einzahl- und eine Mehrzahlform. Man kann eine Zahl davor setzen.		„Uncountable nouns“ bezeichnen z.B. Stoffe (Mehl) oder Gefühle (Liebe), also nicht einzeln greifbare Objekte. Sie haben nur eine Form. Ihnen kann keine Zahl vorangehen.

Siehe 2.6.1 und 2.6.2

Meist ist es klar, welche Substantive zählbar sind und welche nicht. Es gibt aber Fälle, in denen es nicht klar ist, vor allem dann, wenn Wörter in der einen Sprache zählbar, in der anderen nicht zählbar sind. Merken Sie sich vor allem folgende Einträge:

uncountable		**countable**	
bread *I usually eat bread for breakfast.*	Brot	a loaf of bread *Could I have a loaf of bread, please?*	ein (Laib) Brot
fruit *Fruit is non fattening.* *Apples and oranges are fruit.*	Frucht, Früchte	a piece of fruit	eine Frucht
furniture *You have some nice furniture.*	Möbel	a piece of furniture	ein Möbelstück
information *Have you got any information about Britain?* *Information is important.*	Information(en)	a piece of information	eine Information
news *I have some bad news for you.* *Here is the news.*	Nachricht(en)	a piece / an item of news	eine Nachricht
rubbish *We produce a lot of rubbish these days.*	Abfall		
work *I am looking for (some) work.*	Arbeit	a job	eine Arbeit

2.2 Articles (Artikel)

Im Englischen, wie in den meisten westeuropäischen Sprachen, unterscheidet man zwei Arten von Artikeln (auch: Geschlechtswörter genannt), nämlich:
– den unbestimmten Artikel „a/an“ (indefinite article).
– den bestimmten Artikel „the“ (definite article).

2.2.1 Indefinite article

This is a chair.
I have a car.
She's an electrician.
Please come back in an hour.

a happy cat *an unhappy cat*

Es gibt zwei Formen des unbestimmten Artikels: „a“ braucht man, wenn das nächste Wort mit einem Konsonanten beginnt, z.B. b, f, h, s, t, w, y:
a cat, a big cat

„an“ heisst es, wenn das folgende Wort mit einem Vokal (a, e, i, o, u) beginnt:
an apple, an Italian car

Ausnahmen: *an hour, an honest man,*
a university, a uniform

> **Note**
>
> Bei Berufsbezeichnungen wird im Englischen der unbestimmte Artikel verwendet.
> I'm a teacher. nicht: ~~I'm teacher.~~

2.2.2 Definite article

the mother
the father
the child

„Der", „die", „das", sowie „den", „dem" usw. heissen im Englischen immer „the".

> ***Note***
>
> „The" wird auf zwei verschiedene Arten ausgesprochen:
>
> – als [ðə] vor allen Wörtern, denen „a" vorangestellt werden kann:
> the cat   the big cat   the happy cat
>
> – als [ði] vor allen Wörtern, denen „an" vorangestellt werden kann:
> the apple   the 'f'   the umbrella

2.3 Demonstratives: this/that, these/those

„This" wird gebraucht für eine Person oder Sache, „these" für mehrere Personen oder Sachen, die nahe beim Sprechenden ist bzw. sind.
„That" / „those" sagt man, wenn etwas weiter weg ist.
„Demonstratives" können sowohl als Adjektive als auch als Pronomen benutzt werden.

	„here"	**„there"**
Einzahl	This is my bag. This book is blue.	That is your bag. That book is red.
Mehrzahl	These are my shoes. These books are blue.	Those are your shoes. Those books are red.

2.4 Pronouns (Pronomen)

This *is Elizabeth.*
She *is an electrician.*

Das Pronomen (pronoun) steht anstelle des Nomen/Substantiv (noun).
Man verwendet Pronomen, damit man den Namen einer bestimmten Person oder Sache nicht wiederholen muss.

Jim is Antonio's colleague. Antonio invited ***him*** *to dinner.*

2.4.1 Subject and object pronouns

Colleen's from Ireland. She's Irish.
Fritz is from Austria. He's Austrian.
Werner and I are from Switzerland. We're Swiss.
Can you see them?

„Subject pronouns" beantworten die Frage „wer?".
„Object pronouns" beantworten die Frage „wen?" oder „wem?".

Singular	
Subject	**Object**
I you he she it	me you him her it

Plural	
Subject	**Object**
we you they	us you them

Wir benutzen „object pronouns" entweder für
– direkte Objekte:
The policeman saw me in my car.
– oder für indirekte Objekte:
The teacher gave me a book.
– oder nach einer Präposition:
The teacher spoke to me.

Achtung! Auch vor dem Verb „to be" wird ein „object pronoun" gebraucht:
Don't be afraid! It's only me!

2.4.2 Indefinite pronouns (unbestimmte Pronomen)

→ Unit 14

Somebody has sent us a letter.
You don't have to pay anything.
I don't know anybody who doesn't like summer.
There is nothing in this cupboard.
Nobody said anything.

Mit „some“ oder „any“ können unbestimmte Pronomen gebildet werden. Wir beziehen uns damit auf Sachen oder Personen, ohne genau zu sagen, worum oder um wen es sich handelt.

+	- / ?	-
somebody something somewhere	anybody anything anywhere	nobody nothing nowhere

> ***Note***
>
> Beachten Sie die Aussprache von: nothing = [nʌθɪŋ]

Siehe 2.6.1 some/any

> ***Note***
>
> I didn’t eat anything. = I ate nothing.

→ Unit 6, 9

2.4.3 Relative pronouns

A journalist is a person.
\+ A journalist writes articles for a newspaper or magazine.

= A journalist is a person **who** writes articles for a newspaper or magazine.

Yoga is a sport.
\+ Yoga is for breathing and relaxation.

= Yoga is a sport **which** is for breathing and relaxation.

> ***Note***
>
> „Who“ bezieht sich auf Personen.
>
> „Which“ bezieht sich auf Sachen.

People, who live in glass houses shouldn’t throw stones.

2.5 Possessives (Possessivwörter)

2.5.1 Possessive determiners / adjectives

his name

her name

its name

Singular		Plural	
Subject	**Possessive**	**Subject**	**Possessive**
I you he she it	my your his her its	we you they	our your their

Note

Beachten Sie den Unterschied zwischen „its“ und „it's“.
Its name is Socks = Sein Name ist Socks.
It's raining. = It is raining.
It's stopped raining. = It has stopped raining.

Note

„Possessive determiners“ stehen vor Nomen. Im Englischen verändert sich die Form dieser Possessivwörter nicht, wenn das Nomen in der Einzahl oder in der Mehrzahl steht. Zum Beispiel:
My brother lives in Italy.
My parents live in Berne.

2.5.2 's / of

This is Mary's letter.
Antonio is my sister's son.
We will go to my parents' house.
*What's the price **of** this car?*

Um Besitz oder Beziehungen auszudrücken, kann man im Englischen „'s" oder „of" benutzen.

's	Where is Mr Smith's office?	Normalerweise für Personen.
	Children's books	Mehrzahlformen, die nicht auf -s enden
s'	My friends' names are Vikki and Benny.	Wenn Substantive auf -s enden, (z.B. Mehrzahlformen) wird nur ein Apostroph (') eingefügt.
of	The name of the book is „Night Way".	Normalerweise für Dinge.

2.6 Quantifiers (Mengenangaben)

„Quantifiers" gehören wie Artikel zur Klasse der „determiners", also Wörter, die vor Substantiven kommen. Sie sagen etwas über die Menge aus.

→ Unit 3, 14

2.6.1 Some / any / no

Im Deutschen steht bei unbestimmten Mengenangaben kein Artikel. Im Englischen dagegen steht manchmal „some" und manchmal „any".

some	+	There's some orange juice in the fridge. There are some glasses on the table.	*bejahte Sätze*
	?	– Would you like some tea? – Yes, please!	*Angebote und Bitten, wo man ein „ja" als Antwort erwartet*
any	–	We haven't got any mineral water.	*verneinte Sätze mit „not"*
	?	Are there any eggs in the fridge?	*allgemeine Fragen, wo die Antwort nicht voraussehbar ist*
no	–	There are no eggs in the fridge. We've got no mineral water.	*verneinte Sätze*

Note

Die Pronomen „somebody, something, anybody, anything, nobody" etc. folgen obigen Regeln.
Siehe 2.4.2

Note

Im Deutschen gibt es keine Ausdrücke, die „some" und „any" entsprechen. Manchmal werden sie mit „etwas", „einige", „ein paar" übersetzt, meistens aber gar nicht.

→ Unit 3

2.6.2 Much / many / a lot of

„Much" (viel) steht vor „uncountable nouns", „many" (viele) vor „countable nouns" in der Mehrzahl.

Switzerland has lots of tourists.

countable nouns: plural	**uncountable nouns**
many / a lot of / lots of	**much /a lot of / lots of**
How **many** cigarettes do you smoke a day? There are **many /a lot of / lots of** reasons why we cannot travel to Sydney.	How **much** water do you drink a day? I don't eat **much** / **a lot of / lots of** fruit.

Siehe 2.1.2

> *Note*
>
> Mit „much" und „a lot" kann auch ein Vergleich verstärkt werden:
> *I think Jane's old job was much better. – Yes, it was a lot more interesting.*

2.6.3 Both / all

„Both" entspricht dem deutschen „beide", „all" steht für „alle/alles". Folgende Satzmuster sind möglich.

zwei	**mehr als zwei / uncountable**
Both students knew the answer. **Both** of the students knew the answer. **Both** of them knew the answer. They **both** knew the answer. Ian and I **both** like chocolate. They read **both** sides.	**All** (of) the students knew the answer. **All** of them knew the answer. They **all** knew the answer. My friends and I **all** like chocolate. We ate **all** (of) the cake. We ate it **all**. / We **ate** all of it.

2.6.4 Each / every

I go to Italy every / each summer.
Every / each student needs a book.
Take a ball in each hand.
The barcode for each item is ...
Every Sunday is the same.

Sowohl „each“ als auch „every“ können sich auf mehrere Personen oder Dinge beziehen. Sind nur zwei gemeint, muss „each“ verwendet werden:
***Each** of the twins got a present.*

3. Adjectives (Adjektive)

*Fiona has got an **old** car.*
*That's a **lovely** dress. That dress is **lovely**.*
*There's a **comfortable** armchair in the **small** hotel room.*

Adjektive werden gebraucht, um eine Person oder eine Sache näher zu beschreiben. Adjektive heissen auch Eigenschaftswörter, Wiewörter, Beiwörter. Im Englischen haben Adjektive immer die gleiche Form: Es gibt keine Endungen, wie zum Beispiel im Deutschen und Französischen.
Adjektive werden wie im Deutschen entweder vor dem Nomen (*a comfortable armchair*) oder nach Verben wie „to be“ platziert, z.B. *The armchair is / looks comfortable.*

3.1 Comparison of adjectives

→ Unit 4, 10 3.1.1 Comparative and superlative form

*He is **older than** my brother.*
*Max is **bigger than** Paul.*
*Tennis is **more boring than** football.*
*Switzerland is **more expensive than** Germany.*

An elephant has a bigger brain than a man.

Some frogs are more poisonous than snakes.

Um zwei Dinge, Personen oder Gruppen miteinander zu vergleichen, benutzt man den Komparativ (comparative form). Von der Zahl der Silben des Adjektivs hängt ab, ob der Komparativ mit „-er“ (germanische Steigerung) oder mit „more“ (romanische Steigerung) gebildet wird.

Der Superlativ (superlative form) wird gebraucht, um mehr als zwei Dinge, Personen oder Gruppen miteinander zu vergleichen.

Today is the hottest day of the year.
The new CLIK – the easiest way to the Internet.
Tokyo is the most expensive city in the world.
"Angela's Ashes" is the most fascinating book I've ever read.

Germanische Steigerung (wie Deutsch)	**basic form**	**comparative** + er	**superlative** the + est
1-silbige Adjektive	old new	old**er** new**er**	the old**est** the new**est**
Konsonanten-verdoppelung	big hot	big**ger** hot**ter**	the big**gest** the hot**test**
2-silbige Adjektive mit Endung auf -y **y ➪ i**	friendly easy	friendl**ier** eas**ier**	the friendl**iest** the eas**iest**
Romanische Steigerung (wie z.B. Französisch)		more + Adjektiv	the most + Adjektiv
2-silbige und längere Adjektive	important interesting	**more** important **more** interesting	the **most** important the **most** interesting
Unregelmässige Formen			
	good bad	better worse	the best the worst

Note

Achtung:
Max is bigger than Paul. = *Max ist grösser als Paul.*

Note

Mit „much / a lot“ kann auch ein Vergleich verstärkt werden:
I think Jane's old job was **much better**.
A taxi is **much more expensive** than a bus.

4. Adverbs (Adverbien)

The time passed very quickly.
Do you often see him?
The film was quite exciting.

Adverbien beschreiben, wie, wann, wie oft, wo oder unter welchen Umständen etwas geschieht.

Sie geben Antwort auf Fragen wie:
– how? *The alarm rang **loudly**.*
– how often? *They **never** visited us.*

Sie können aber auch zusammen mit Adjektiven verwendet werden:
– ***very** good*
– ***extremely** fast*

oder mit einem anderen Adverb:
– ***very** often*

→ Unit 8

4.1 Adverbs of frequency

„Adverbs of frequency" geben Antwort auf die Frage „wie oft" (how often?, how many times?).

*I **always** surf the Internet before I have breakfast.*
*I **sometimes** have an afternoon nap.*
*I **usually** go shopping after work.*

He has never eaten a hamburger.

never	sometimes now and then seldom	usually normally often regularly	always
0%			100%

She always has breakfast in bed.

Position

„Adverbs of frequency" stehen gewöhnlich direkt **vor** dem Hauptverb.

I	*always*	*get up*	*at 6.30.*
She has	*never*	*been*	*to India.*
My colleagues	*usually*	*have lunch*	*in the canteen.*

Ausnahme: mit dem Verb „be" stehen die Adverbien nach „am/are/is/was/were".

They	*were*	*always*	*early.*
Valentine's Day	*is*	*always*	*on February 14th.*
There	*are*	*often*	*Halloween parties in schools.*

4.2 Adverbs of manner

*She sang **happily** in her bath.*
*The children ate the hamburgers **quickly**.*
*I **carefully** turned the switch.*
*She sings **beautifully**.*
*The child asked **politely** for some more food.*
*She plays the piano very **well**.*

„Adverbs of manner" beschreiben, wie etwas gemacht wird („manner" = Art und Weise).

	Adjektiv	**Adverb**
Adjektiv + **ly**	slow urgent excited	slow**ly** urgent**ly** excited**ly**
Adjektive auf -y: **y** ➪ **i** + **ly**	easy necessary	eas**ily** necessar**ily**
Adjektive auf -le: **-le** ➪ **-ly**	terrible suitable gentle	terrib**ly** suitab**ly** gent**ly**

Ausnahmen:

fast	fast
good	well
hard	hard
true	truly
whole	wholly
automatic	automatically*
basic	basically*
	*das eingeschobene „a" wird nicht ausgesprochen.

She plays the piano very well.

Note

Aufgepasst beim Übersetzen:
Sie ist schön. = She is beautiful.
Sie singt schön. = She sings beautifully.

She's beautiful, but she doesn't sing beautifully.

Position

„Adverbs of manner“ stehen gewöhnlich am Ende des Satzes oder vor dem Hauptverb.

They	*ate*	*slowly.*
He	*finished his work*	*quickly.*
The policeman	*looked at the paper*	*carefully.*
The train	*slowly*	*came round the bend.*
I'm	*slowly*	*beginning to understand.*
I'll	*briefly*	*explain what has happened.*

5. Prepositions

*I work **at** an airport.*
*The meeting is **at** three o'clock.*
*I've lived here **for** five years.*
*The bus station is **on** the left.*

Präpositionen (prepositions) stehen meist vor einem Nomen (noun) bzw. Pronomen (pronoun). Präpositionen dienen häufig dazu, Ort oder Zeit auszudrücken. Sie lassen sich nicht 1:1 ins Deutsche übersetzen und sollten deshalb immer im Zusammenhang gelernt werden.

5.1 Prepositions of time (Zeit)

→ Unit 2, 4

Zeit	at	The meeting is at three o'clock. / at night.	um drei Uhr / in der Nacht
	for	I've lived here for five years.	seit fünf Jahren
	since	I've lived here since 2001.	seit 2001
	on	I work on Friday.	am Freitag
	in	I work in the afternoon.	am Nachmittag
	ago	I came here 3 years ago.	vor 3 Jahren

→ Unit 4

5.2 Prepositions of place and movement (Ort und Bewegung)

Alice is sitting in the water.
Ben is jumping into/in the water.
Colin is getting out of the water.
Denise is inside the playhouse.
Ernie is outside the playhouse.
Frank is on the playhouse.

Georgina is jumping off the playhouse.
Helen is going down the slide.
Ian is going up the steps.
Janet is hiding under the slide.
Ken is sitting in front of Linda.
Linda is sitting behind Ken.
Mike is sitting behind Nina.
Nina is sitting opposite / across from Ken.
Owen is standing beside / next to the slide.
Pat is climbing through the pipe.
Quentin is jumping over the rope.
Robert is running round the tree.
Sally is leaning against the tree.
Tom is throwing the ball to Ursula.
Ursula is standing near the water.
Valerie is walking across the path.
Wendy is walking along the path past the swing.
Xavier is running from the playhouse towards the gate.
Yvonne is at/by the gate.
Zachary is walking away from it all.
The cat is jumping onto the playhouse.
The dog is sitting on the log.

Between the lake and the mountain, among the trees.

I work at the airport / at home.
Can you tell me the way to the post office?

6. Sentences (der Satz)

6.1 Question words ('wh'-questions)

6.1.1 When / where / why

***When** is your English class?*
***When** did he go to Australia?*
***Where** do you live?*
***Where** are they from?*
***Why** haven't you done the exercise?*

Das Fragewort steht zuerst, danach folgt der Satz in der Frageform.

Mit „when" fragt man danach, „wann" etwas geschehen ist oder geschehen wird.

Mit „where" fragt man nach dem „wo". Mit „where ... to/from" fragt man nach dem „wohin" bzw. „woher", wobei „to" und „from" am Ende des Satzes stehen.

Where is the classroom?	Wo ist das Klassenzimmer?
Where do you come from?	Woher kommst du?
Where are you going to?	Wohin gehst du?

Note

Es gibt mehrere Fragewörter, die mit „wh" beginnen. Zwei davon sind für Deutschsprachige nicht einfach auseinander zu halten.

„who?" = wer?
„where?" = wo?

→ Unit 4

6.1.2 How

„How“ kann allein am Anfang des Satzes stehen oder zusammen mit einem Adjektiv oder Adverb (z.B. How long?, How many?, How fast?).

***How** are you?*
***How** do you say this in English?*
***How long** have you lived in Zurich?*
***How many** colleagues do you have?*
***How much** time do you have?*
***How often** do you go on holiday?*

6.1.3 Who / what

„Who“ braucht man für Personen, „what“ für Sachen.

***What** is your name?*
***What** do you do?*
***Who** is your boss?*
***Who's** that?*

> *Note*
> who = wer
> what = was, wie

6.1.4 Which / what

*You can have a red, a blue or a green pen. **Which** colour would you like?*

*I'd like to ask you some questions about your likes and dislikes. **What** is your favourite colour? **What** sort of house do you live in? **What** book are you reading at the moment? **What** television programmes do you watch?*

***Which** boy on this photo is your son?*

„What“ wird für Sachen gebraucht, „which“ für Sachen oder Personen. „Which“ ist für eine eingeschränkte Auswahl von Sachen und „what“ für eine grössere Auswahl. Beide Wörter können allein stehen oder zusammen mit einem Substantiv.

7. Appendix (Anhang)

7.1 List of irregular verbs

infinitive	past simple	past participle
be	was/were	been
beat	beat	beaten
break	broke	broken
bring	brought	brought
build	built	built
buy	bought	bought
choose	chose	chosen
come	came	come
do	did	done
draw	drew	drawn
dream	dreamt	dreamt
drink	drank	drunk
drive	drove	driven
eat	ate	eaten
feel	felt	felt
fight	fought	fought
fly	flew	flown
get	got	got
give	gave	given
go	went	gone
grow	grew	grown
have	had	had
hear	heard	heard
keep	kept	kept
learn	learnt	learnt
leave	left	left
let	let	let
lose	lost	lost
make	made	made
meet	met	met
pay	paid	paid
put	put	put
read	read	read
ride	rode	ridden
run	run	run
say	said	said
see	saw	seen
sell	sold	sold
send	sent	sent
sing	sang	sung

infinitive	past simple	past participle
sit sleep speak spend stand swim take tell think throw wear win write	sat slept spoke spent stood swam took told thought threw wore won wrote	sat slept spoken spent stood swum taken told thought thrown worn won written

7.2 Verb patterns

➜ Unit 10, 12

agree	I **agree with** you. I think we should all **agree to** work together.
answer	Please **answer my question**. **Answer me** when I ask you a question.
apply	I'm going to **apply for** a new job.
ask	**Ask me a question!** He went into a pub and **asked for** a beer. / He met a neighbour and **asked about** her family. / She **asked** him **to** help her with a problem.
be afraid	Are you **afraid of** flying? **I'm afraid** I can't come to your party. Please excuse me!
begin	I opened the book and I **began** read**ing / to** read.
come	My brother just **came back** from Australia. **Come in** and have a cup of tea! The tea **comes from** India.
cope	Can you **cope with** the stress?

depend	Children **depend on** their parents.
enjoy	Do you **enjoy** danc**ing**? – Yes, but I **enjoy** the music more.
get	It was a great day! First I **got up**, then I **got dressed**. After that, I **got the bus** to town. When I **got to** town, the weather **was getting warme**r. I **got** a coffee in a café and then I **got to know** this beautiful woman. We **got married** three months later!
give	I **give up**! I can't find the answer to the question. Can you **give** me some help?
go	Yesterday I **went out**. I **went to** town. As the day **went on**, I became hungry. I saw a nice restaurant and **went in**. I didn't know what to have, but in the end I **went for** fish.
grow	When I **was growing up** in the country, we used to **grow vegetables** in the garden.
like	Would you **like to** dance? – I'm afraid I can't. I **like** danc**ing**, but I've hurt my foot.
look	Can you help me? I'm **looking for** my keys. – What do they **look like**? You should **look after** them better and then you wouldn't lose them! Have you **looked in** all your bags?
look forward	I **look forward to** your reply. I **look forward to** see**ing** you next week.
marry	She said: „Will you **marry me**?" I said yes. We **got married** in September. We had a big wedding. Now we **have been married** for two years.
need	I'm thirsty. I **need** a glass of water. – You **needn't get up**, I'll get you a glass.
prevent	The bad weather **prevented** us **from** go**ing** out.

promise	She **promised to** help me tomorrow.
put	I **put on** my coat and **put** my keys in my pocket. My friend **put on** three kilograms during the holidays.
rely	You can **rely on** the Swiss railways.
remind	**Remind** me **to** go to the bank today. The photo **reminded** me **of** my holidays.
sit	I **sat down** on the sofa and then I **sat** there for 2 hours.
speak	Can you **speak** Spanish? We **spoke with** our teacher **about** holidays.
spend	I **spent** a lot of time and money **on** my English course.
stand	The class **stood up** when the teacher came in. The train was so full, I had to **stand** all the way to Berne.
stop	When did you **stop** smok**ing**? While they were shopping, they **stopped to** have a cup of coffee.
take	Last week I **took** a flight to London. When I got in the plane, I **took off** my coat and sat down. The plane **took off**. The flight **took** $1\frac{1}{2}$ hours. In London I went to a concert which **took place** in a park.
tell	**Tell me a story**. **Tell me about** your time in Australia. The teacher **told us to** open our books.
try	I **tried to** call you, but you weren't there. I had a bad cold, so I **tried** drink**ing** lots of tea, but it didn't help. Chantal **tried on** a coat in the new clothes shop.
turn	Use the switch to **turn** the computer **on** and **off**. **Turn right** at the lights and then **turn left** by the bank.

7.3 Numbers

1	one	11	eleven	20	twenty	21	twenty-one
2	two	12	twelve	30	thirty	32	thirty-two
3	three	13	thirteen	40	forty	43	forty-three
4	four	14	fourteen	50	fifty	54	fifty-four
5	five	15	fifteen	60	sixty	65	sixty-five
6	six	16	sixteen	70	seventy	76	seventy-six
7	seven	17	seventeen	80	eighty	87	eighty-seven
8	eight	18	eighteen	90	ninety	98	ninety-eight
9	nine	19	nineteen	100	a hundred	109	a hundred and nine
10	ten						

Note

four	fourteen	forty
five	fifteen	fifty

7.4 Ordinal numbers

first	1st	seventh	7th	thirteenth	13th
second	2nd	eighth	8th	fifteenth	15th
third	3rd	ninth	9th	twentieth	20th
fourth	4th	tenth	10th	twenty-first	21st
fifth	5th	eleventh	11th	fiftieth	50th
sixth	6th	twelfth	12th	hundredth	100th

7.5 Telling the time (clock)

Note

Aufgepasst mit „half“.
Man sagt im Englischen „halb nach“!

half past two = halb drei
half past three = halb vier

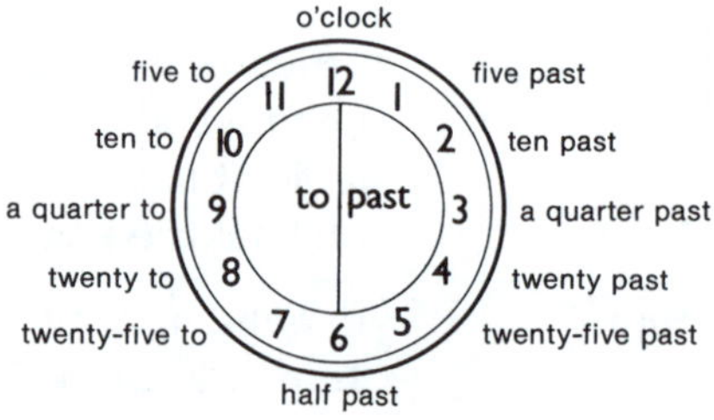

Sorry, what time is it?

8. Communication

8.1 Giving directions

Asking the way

● Excuse me, can you tell me the way to the post office?
▼ Yes, of course. Turn left at the coffee shop. Walk to the end of the street and it's on your right.

● Excuse me, which floor is Mr Fitzgerald's office on?
▼ It's on the fourth floor. You can take the lift.

Telling the way

– Turn left (at the end of the road).
– Turn right.
– Go/Walk to the end of the street.
– The (post office) is on the right/left.
– Walk down the road for (200) metres.

– It's on the (4th) floor.
– You can take the lift (GB) / elevator (US) or the stairs.

If you don't understand you can say:
– Pardon/Sorry? (GB) / Excuse me? (US)
– I'm sorry, I didn't understand.
– Can you say that again?
– Can you speak more slowly?

If you want to check that you have understood you can repeat what you heard, e.g:

● Turn left at the lights.
▼ Turn left at the lights?
● Yes, that's right.

8.2 Social situations

- ● Would you like a cup of coffee?
- ▼ Yes, please.
- ● With cream and sugar?
- ▼ Cream please, no sugar.
- ● Here you are.
- ▼ Thank you very much.
- ● You're welcome.

- ● Would you like to go to the cinema on Thursday?
- ▼ Yes, that's a good idea. Where shall we meet?
- ● Why don't we meet at the pub at 7 o'clock?
- ▼ OK. See you then.

- ● Would you like to go out on Friday night?
- ▼ I'm sorry, I'm working late on Friday.
- ● Well, how about going dancing on Saturday?

8.3 Telephoning

- ● Hello?
- ▼ Hello, is that Sarah?
- ● Yes, this is Sarah speaking.
- ▼ Hi, this is Paul.
- ● Oh, hello, how are you?

- ▼ Hello?
- ● This is Sonia. Is that Laura?
- ▼ No, this is Sarah. Laura's not here.
- ● Oh, can I leave a message?
- ▼ Of course.

- ● BCS International. How can I help you?
- ▼ Could I speak to Jim Smith, please?
- ● Who's calling please?
- ▼ This is Antonio Graf.
- ● Just one moment, Mr Graf. I'll put you through.
- ▼ Thank you.

Wenn Sie Schwierigkeiten am Telefon haben, benutzen Sie die folgenden Ausdrücke:

- I'm sorry, I didn't catch/understand that.
- Sorry, could you repeat that?
- Could you speak a little more slowly?
- Can you spell that, please?
- Let me check if I've got that right.

9. Vocabulary – unit by unit

Lautschrift und Beispielwörter:

[:] Ein Doppelpunkt bedeutet, dass ein vorhergehender Laut lang ausgesprochen wird.

['] Betonungszeichen oben: Die Hauptbetonung liegt auf der folgenden Silbe.

[ˌ] Betonungszeichen unten: Die Nebenbetonung liegt auf der folgenden Silbe.

[‿] Ein Bogen unter Lauten bedeutet, dass die Laute zusammengezogen werden bei der Aussprache.

Die Lautschrift folgt Jones, English Pronouncing Dictionary, 15th edition.

Die angegebene Aussprache ist britisch. Die regionalen und länderspezifischen Unterschiede äussern sich in erster Linie in der Aussprache der Vokale.

[ʌ]	bus	[bʌs]	[ɪ]	it	[ɪt]	[ŋ]	young	[jʌŋ]
[ɑ]	last	[lɑ:st]	[ɪə]	here	[hɪə]	[r]	friend	[frend]
[aɪ]	my	[maɪ]	[i:]	please	[pli:z]	[s]	sir	[sɜ:]
[aʊ]	how	[haʊ]	[ɒ]	not	[nɒt]	[z]	busy	['bɪzɪ]
[æ]	back	[bæk]	[ɔ]	boy	[bɔɪ]	[θ]	both	[bəʊθ]
[e]	next	[nekst]	[ɔ:]	all	[ɔ:l]	[ð]	that	[ðæt]
[eɪ]	name	[neɪm]	[ʊ]	book	[bʊk]	[ʃ]	shop	[ʃɒp]
[eə]	where	[weə]	[ʊə]	tourist	[tʊərɪst]	[ʒ]	television	['telɪvɪʒn]
[ə]	member	['membə]	[u:]	who	[hu:]	[v]	visit	['vɪzɪt]
[əʊ]	own	[əʊn]				[w]	well	[wel]
[ɜ]	word	[wɜ:d]				[tʃ]	church	[tʃɜ:tʃ]
						[dʒ]	Germany	['dʒɜ:mənɪ]

Unit 1

1

to get to know [ˌget tə 'nəʊ]	I'd like to get to know him.	kennen lernen
interests ['ɪntrəsts]	What are your interests?	Interessen
to introduce [ˌɪntrə'dju:s]	I'd like to introduce Oliver to you.	vorstellen
occupation [ˌɒkju'peɪʃn]	What's your occupation?	Beruf
pet [pet]	My daughter has a pet rabbit.	Haustier
question ['kwestʃn]	What's your question?	Frage
sentence ['sentəns]	Write a complete sentence.	Satz
size [saɪz]	My shoe size is 42.	Grösse
to spell [spel]	Can you spell your name?	buchstabieren
true [tru:]	The story is true.	wahr
yourself [jɔ:'self]	The information is about yourself.	dich selbst

2

actor ['æktə]	Sean Connery is an actor.	Schauspieler
answer ['ɑ:nsə]	The answer is wrong.	Antwort
chess [tʃes]	Can you play chess?	Schach
collection [kə'lekʃn]	Look at his collection of stamps.	Sammlung
to compare [kəm'peə]	Compare your answers with your partner.	vergleichen
description [dɪ'skɪpʃn]	Write a description.	Beschreibung
dictionary ['dɪkʃənri]	Look up the word in your dictionary.	Wörterbuch
each other [i:tʃ 'ʌðə]	We write to each other about twice a year.	gegenseitig
famous ['feɪməs]	Madonna is a famous person.	berühmt

to look like ['lʊk laɪk]	What does he look like?	aussehen
memory ['meməri]	You have a good memory.	Gedächtnis
politician [ˌpɒlə'tɪʃn]	He's a politician.	Politiker
prison ['prɪzn]	If you are in prison, you're not free.	Gefängnis
sex [seks]	What is the baby's sex?	Geschlecht
to throw [θrəʊ]	Throw a ball to another student.	werfen
wrong [rɒŋ]	I think that's wrong.	falsch

3

change [tʃeɪndʒ]	The new job was a big change for me.	Wechsel, Veränderung
main [meɪn]	Do you understand the main points?	Haupt-
point [pɔɪnt]	What's the main point?	Punkt
result [rɪ'zʌlt]	Tell the class your results.	Ergebnis

4

arrival [ə'raɪvl]	We are waiting for their arrival.	Ankunft
attractive [ə'træktɪv]	It's an attractive place.	attraktiv
capital ['kæpɪtl]	Valletta is the capital of Malta.	Hauptstadt
century ['sentʃri]	Malta's temples were built over several centuries.	Jahrhundert
clear [klɪə]	The sea is clear.	klar
climate ['klaɪmət]	Do you think the climate has changed?	Klima
colony ['kɒləni]	Malta was a British colony.	Kolonie
to date back [ˌdeɪt 'bæk]	The temple dates back to 4000 BC.	stammt aus der Zeit
departure [dɪ'pɑːtʃə]	When is your departure?	Abfahrt, Abflug

destination [ˌdestɪ'neɪʃn]	Malta is an ideal holiday destination.	hier: Urlaubsort, -ziel
few [fju:]	There are very few cold days.	wenig
to fit [fɪt]	Does the answer fit the question?	(zu etwas) passen
fog [fɒg]	They have almost no fog on Malta.	Nebel
to go sightseeing ['saɪtsi:ɪŋ]	We go sightseeing for one full day a week.	besichtigen
healthy ['helθi]	The climate is healthy.	gesund
heritage ['herətɪdʒ]	The temples are our heritage.	Erbe
independent [ˌɪndə'pendənt]	Malta became independent in 1964.	unabhängig
island ['aɪlənd]	Malta is an island.	Insel
knight [naɪt]	The knights in Malta built many palaces.	Ritter
magnificent [mæg'nɪfɪsnt]	The temples are magnificent.	grossartig
Mediterranean [ˌmedɪtə'reɪniən]	Malta lies in the Mediterranean.	Mittelmeer
population [ˌpɒpju'leɪʃn]	The population of Malta is 50,000.	Einwohnerzahl
prehistoric [ˌpri:hɪ'strɒrɪk]	Malta has many prehistoric temples.	prähistorisch
pub [pʌb]	There are many English pubs on Malta.	Kneipe
several ['sevrəl]	There are several very old temples.	mehrere
situated ['sɪtʃueɪtid]	Malta is situated in the Mediterranean.	gelegen
village ['vɪlɪdʒ]	I like the little fishing village.	Dorf
wet [wet]	January is usually wet.	nass

5

heading ['hedɪŋ]	The list has a heading: Food.	Überschrift
paragraph ['pærəgrɑ:f]	There are five paragraphs in the text.	Absatz
to put [pʊt]	Put the cup on the table.	stellen

6

bank transfer ['bæŋk ˌtrænsfɜː]	I'll pay by bank transfer.	Banküberweisung
box [bɒks]	Fill in the box on the form.	Kasten
centre ['sentə]	The school is in the centre of town.	Zentrum
to choose [tʃuːz]	Choose a picture.	auswählen
to complete [kəm'pliːt]	Complete the sentence.	vervollständigen
date of birth [deɪt əv bɜːθ]	What's your date of birth?	Geburtsdatum
to decide [dɪ'saɪd]	Decide which words are important.	(sich) entscheiden
duration [dju'reɪʃn]	The duration of the course is 2 weeks.	Dauer
to fill in [fɪl 'ɪn]	Fill in the information on the form.	ausfüllen
form [fɔːm]	Fill in the registration form.	Formular
full board [ˌfʊl 'bɔːd]	I booked full board.	Vollpension
host family ['həʊst ˌfæməli]	You can stay with a host family.	Gastfamilie
individual [ˌɪndɪ'vɪdʒuəl]	I booked individual lessons.	Einzel-, einzelne
to participate [pɑː'tɪsɪpeɪt]	You can participate in the programme.	teilnehmen
payment ['peɪmənt]	The payment is made by cheque.	Zahlung
postcode ['pəustkəud]	What's the post code for Vienna?	Postleitzahl
registration [ˌredʒɪ'streɪʃn]	Fill in the registration form.	Anmeldung
signature ['sɪgnətʃə]	Write your signature on the form.	Unterschrift
single ['sɪŋgl]	Don't try to understand every single word.	einzeln
to sum up [ˌsʌm 'ʌp]	That sums up your arguments.	zusammenfassen

7

afraid of [ə'freɪd]	I'm afraid of making mistakes.	Angst haben vor
difficult ['dɪfɪkəlt]	Do you find English difficult to learn?	schwierig

difficulty ['dɪfɪkəlti]	the difficulty of speaking English	Schwierigkeit
meaning ['mi:nɪŋ]	What's the meaning of that word?	Bedeutung
to mention ['menʃn]	Can I mention your name?	erwähnen
mistake [mɪ'steɪk]	I made a mistake.	Fehler
to practise ['præktɪs]	You need to practise.	üben
to pronounce [prə'naʊns]	English is difficult to pronounce.	aussprechen
to tick [tɪk]	Tick the words that you hear.	abhaken
to translate [træn'sleɪt]	I try to translate everything.	übersetzen

8

cook [kʊk]	He works as a cook in a restaurant.	Koch
to dive [daɪv]	I like to dive off the 10-metre board.	tauchen
foreign ['fɒrən]	I speak two foreign languages.	fremd

Unit 2

1

amber ['æmbə]	The traffic lights are red, green and amber.	(Verkehrsampel) gelb; bernsteinfarben
ambulance ['æmbjələns]	Call 999 for an ambulance in England.	Ambulanz
cheek [tʃi:k]	You have the cheek to think you're better.	hier: Frechheit
coloured ['kʌləd]	It's not right to call him coloured.	farbig
to develop [dɪ'veləp]	You can develop your word wheel each week.	entwickeln
dialect ['daɪəlekt]	I cannot speak the Australian dialect.	Dialekt

necessary ['nesəsri]	Use a dictionary if necessary.	nötig
object ['ɒbdʒekt]	What colour is the following object?	Gegenstand
rainbow ['reɪnbəʊ]	I love all the colours of the rainbow.	Regenbogen
scared [skɛəd]	I feel scared when I am alone.	Angst haben
sunset ['sʌnset]	I love the sunsets in summer.	Sonnenuntergang
traffic lights ['træfɪk laɪts]	The traffic lights are green, amber and red.	Ampel
watermelon ['wɔːtəˌmeln]	Watermelons are red on the inside.	Wassermelone
wheel [wiːl]	Write the words in a word wheel.	Rad

2

actions ['ækʃnz]	His actions are different from his words.	Handlungen
aggression [ə'greʃn]	Red is often the colour of aggression.	Aggression
author ['ɔːθə]	The author of the poem is unknown.	Schriftsteller, Autor, -in
boredom ['bɔːdəm]	Grey is the colour of boredom.	Langeweile
choice [tʃɔɪs]	Compare your choice of colour.	Auswahl
colourful ['kʌləfəl]	He speaks in a colourful way.	farbenfroh, bunt
death [deθ]	In Europe, black is the colour of death.	Tod
depressed [dɪ'prest]	He is sometimes depressed.	deprimiert
depression [dɪ'preʃn]	More and more people suffer from depression.	Depression
to describe [dɪ'skraɪb]	Can you describe where you live?	beschreiben
to express [ɪk'spres]	Colours express our feelings.	ausdrücken
to feel blue [fiːl 'bluː]	John is feeling blue because his girlfriend has left him.	traurig sein
feelings ['fiːlɪŋz]	I don't like talking about my feelings.	Gefühle
feminine ['femɪnɪn]	This is a feminine style.	weiblich
happiness ['hæpinəs]	Orange is the colour of happiness.	Glück

masculine ['mæskjəlɪn]	Blue is a masculine colour to a lot of people.	männlich
mood [mu:d]	He's in a black mood.	Laune, Stimmung
piece [pi:s]	Listen to this piece of music.	Stück
to represent [ˌreprə'zent]	White represents death in Asian countries.	stehen für
to see red [si: 'red]	My dad saw red when I came home late.	rot sehen
way [weɪ]	He speaks in a colourful way.	hier: Art
wedding ['wedɪn]	She wore a white wedding dress.	Hochzeit

3

adjective ['ædʒəktɪv]	'Hot' and 'short' are adjectives.	Eigenschaftswort
curly ['kɜ:li]	She has curly hair.	lockig
elderly ['eldəli]	He's an elderly gentleman.	älterer
height [haɪt]	What height are you?	Körpergrösse
kind [kaɪnd]	Thank you. You're very kind.	liebenswürdig, freundlich
lazy ['leɪzi]	She is not lazy at all.	faul
medium ['mi:diəm]	She is of medium height.	mittlere/-r
middle-aged [ˌmɪdl 'eɪdʒd]	He's middle-aged.	mittleren Alters
odd one out [ˌɒd wʌn 'aʊt]	Circle the odd one out.	etwas, das nicht dazu gehört
pretty ['prɪti]	She's very pretty.	hübsch
red-headed [red'hedɪd]	Fiona is red-headed.	rothaarig
sad [sæd]	Why are you looking sad?	traurig
shirt [ʃɜ:t]	I always wear a white shirt to work.	Hemd, Bluse
slim [slɪm]	She's tall and slim.	schlank
straight [streɪt]	She's got straight hair.	glatt
tall [tɔ:l]	Vanessa is quite tall.	gross

thin [θɪn]	The singer is thin.	dünn
well-built [ˌwel 'bɪlt]	Mr Brant is tall and well-built.	kräftig

5

at the age of [eɪdʒ]	She had her first lesson at the age of 5.	im Alter von
beauty ['bju:ti]	Vanessa is a young beauty.	Schönheit
frozen ['frəʊzn]	The lake was frozen last winter.	(zu-)gefroren
lake [leɪk]	The lake in St. Moritz was frozen.	(der) See
later on ['leɪtər‿ɒn]	Vanessa would like to study later on.	später
magic ['mædʒɪk]	Music is like magic.	Zauber
to marry ['mæri]	Will she marry him?	heiraten
to move [mu:v]	Vanessa moved to London.	umziehen
to perform [pə'fɔ:m]	She performed in St. Moritz.	aufführen
phrase [freɪz]	A phrase is a part of a sentence.	Satzteil
regularly ['regjələli]	She doesn't go to school regularly.	regelmässig
signpost ['saɪnpəust]	The signpost shows the way.	Wegweiser
sky [skaɪ]	The sky is full of stars.	Himmel
solicitor [sə'lɪsətə]	She married a solicitor.	Rechtsanwalt
tutor ['tju:tə]	Vanessa has a private tutor.	Hauslehrer
to underline [ˌʌndə'laɪn]	Underline all the words.	unterstreichen
violin [ˌvaɪə'lɪn]	She plays the violin.	Geige
violinist [ˌvaɪə'lɪnɪst]	Vanessa is a violinist.	Geiger/-in
world [wɜ:ld]	She travelled all over the world.	Welt

7

amount [ə'maʊnt]	£100,000 is a large amount of money.	Menge
to cause [kɔ:z]	Some people caused trouble at the festival.	verursachen
chaos ['keɪɒs]	The bad weather caused chaos at the festival.	Chaos
charity ['tʃærəti]	The 'Red Cross' is a famous charity.	wohltätige Organisation
crowd [kraʊd]	There were big crowds at the festival.	Menschenmenge
edition [ɪ'dɪʃn]	On today's edition of the programme ...	Ausgabe
event [ɪ'vent]	There are many outdoor events in summer.	Veranstaltung
farm [fɑ:m]	There were many animals on the farm.	Farm
festival ['festəvl]	There is a jazz festival in Montreux each year.	Festival
field [fi:ld]	The farmer has four fields.	Feld
future ['fju:tʃə]	Do you have any plans for the future?	Zukunft
gatecrasher ['geɪtkræʃə]	Gatecrashers go to a party but they don't have tickets.	ungeladener Gast
last [lɑ:st]	The festival lasts three days.	dauern
local community [ˌləʊkl ˌkə'mju:nəti]	The local community don't like all the tourists.	örtliche Gemeinschaft
market stall ['mɑ:kɪt stɔ:l]	I bought some jeans from the market stall.	Marktstand
mud [mʌd]	Don't come in. You have mud all over your shoes.	Dreck
nearby [ˌnɪə'baɪ]	There's a good restaurant nearby.	in der Nähe
noise [nɔɪz]	I can't hear you, there's too much noise.	Lärm
outdoor ['aʊtdɔ:]	In summer I go to the outdoor swimming pool.	im Freien, draussen
owner ['əʊnə]	Are you the owner of this car?	Besitzer
party-goer ['pɑ:tigəʊə]	There were lots of party-goers in the streets.	Partygänger/-in
permit ['pɜ:mɪt]	Some people need a permit to work in Switzerland.	Erlaubnis
profit ['prɒfɪt]	The festival made a big profit.	Gewinn
rubbish ['rʌbɪʃ]	There was rubbish everywhere.	Abfall, Dreck
security [sɪ'kjʊərəti]	The bank has good security.	Sicherheit

stage [steɪdʒ]	The actor came onto the stage.	Bühne
to take off [ˌteɪk 'ɒf]	The event took off in 1981.	beginnen
to take place [ˌteɪk 'pleɪs]	The festival takes place every summer.	stattfinden
uncertain [ˌʌn'sɜ:tn]	The future is always uncertain.	unsicher

Unit 3

3

carton ['kɑ:tn]	I bought two cartons of milk.	Karton
cookie (US) ['kʊki]	Do you want a cookie?	Keks
dozen ['dʌzn]	There are twelve in a dozen.	Dutzend
fridge [frɪdʒ]	The milk is in the fridge.	Kühlschrank
juice [dʒu:s]	I drink orange juice every day.	Saft
peach [pi:tʃ]	You need peaches for the fruit salad.	Pfirsich
tin [tɪn]	You can buy peaches in a tin.	Dose

4

assistant [ə'sɪstənt]	Where is the shop assistant?	Verkäufer/in
customer ['kʌstəmə]	The shop is full of customers.	Kunde
else [els]	Do you want anything else?	noch (etwas)
kind [kaɪnd]	"Bangra" is a kind of Indian music.	Art

5

to count [kaʊnt]	Can you count the number of words?	zählen
lifestyle ['laɪfstaɪl]	Do you have a healthy lifestyle?	Lebensstil
once [wʌns]	I play tennis once a week.	einmal
twice [twaɪs]	I play tennis twice a week.	zweimal
vegetable ['vedʒtəbl]	I eat only vegetables.	Gemüse

6

bride [braɪd]	The bride wore a white wedding dress.	Braut
ceremony ['serəməni]	The wedding ceremony was only 20 minutes.	Zeremonie
column ['kɒləm]	Put the words in the right column.	Spalte
countess ['kaʊntes]	I read a story about the Countess of York.	Gräfin
couple ['kʌpl]	The young couple flew to Paris.	Paar
to cut [kʌt]	They cut the cake with a big knife.	schneiden
to decorate ['dekəreɪt]	I decorated the tables with flowers.	schmücken
decoration [ˌdekə'reɪʃn]	I put the flower decoration on the table.	Dekoration
department store [dɪ'pɑ:tmənt stɔ:]	There are many department stores in Zurich.	Kaufhaus, Warenhaus
dessert [dɪ'zɜ:t]	I'd like ice cream for dessert.	Nachtisch
dinner ['dɪnə]	I'd like to invite you for dinner.	Abendessen
dish [dɪʃ]	Can you name a local dish?	Gericht
fairy-tale ['feəriteɪl]	The wedding ceremony was like in a fairy-tale.	Märchen
held [held]	The wedding is held at the family home.	stattfinden
honey ['hʌni]	I put honey in my tea.	Honig
honeymoon ['hʌnimu:n]	They went to Paris for their honeymoon.	Flitterwochen
to include [ɪn'klu:d]	The list includes all my friends.	einschliessen

to invite [ɪn'vaɪt]	I'd like to invite you for dinner.	einladen
lamb [læm]	We had roast lamb for dinner.	Lamm
plate [pleɪt]	Rosenthal plates are expensive.	Teller
plural ['plʊərəl]	'Boys' is the plural of 'boy'.	Mehrzahl
relatives ['relətɪvs]	I have relatives in the States: two sisters.	Verwandte
selection [sə'lekʃn]	There was a large selection of vegetables.	Auswahl
to serve [sɜːv]	I served brown bread with the smoked salmon.	hier: servieren
smoked ['sməʊkt]	I had a sandwich with smoked salmon.	geräuchert
sword [sɔːd]	A knight carried a sword.	Schwert
unknown [ˌʌn'nəʊn]	Their destination is unknown.	unbekannt
wealthy ['welθi]	He's very wealthy.	wohlhabend

7

to add [æd]	Can you add a word to the list?	hinzufügen
to chop [tʃɒp]	Chop the onion!	klein schneiden, hacken
cream cheese [ˌkriːm 'tʃiːz]	You make cheesecake with cream cheese.	Frischkäse
crisps [krɪsps]	We need five packets of crisps.	Kartoffelchips
finely ['faɪnli]	Chop the onion finely.	fein, klein
to grate [greɪt]	Grate the apples.	reiben
instruction [ɪn'strʌkʃn]	The instructions are clear.	Anweisung
lemon ['lemən]	I drink tea with lemon.	Zitrone
to mix [mɪks]	Mix the cheese with the mayonnaise.	mischen
to need [niːd]	You need a ticket to travel on the train.	benötigen, brauchen
pepper ['pepə]	Add pepper and salt to the dish.	Pfeffer
raisin ['reɪzn]	The cake was full of raisins.	Rosine

recipe ['resəpi]	Can you give me the recipe?	Rezept
salt [sɔ:lt]	I like a lot of salt on my chips.	Salz

8

company ['kʌmpəni]	He's visiting an American company.	Firma
to explain [ɪk'spleɪn]	She can explain it to me later.	erklären
meal [mi:l]	Let's go for a meal.	Essen, Mahlzeit
speciality [ˌspeʃi'æləti]	The local speciality is rabbit and polenta.	Spezialität

Unit 4

1

behind [bɪ'haɪnd]	There is a garden behind the house.	hinter
between [bɪ'twi:n]	My car is between the red car and the blue car.	zwischen
bin [bɪn]	The bin is under the desk.	Papierkorb
calculator ['kælkjuleɪtə]	I bought a new calculator.	Taschenrechner
desk [desk]	My desk is in the centre of the room.	Schreibtisch
drawing ['drɔ:ɪn]	I can make a drawing of my house.	Zeichnung
equipment [ɪ'kwɪpmənt]	The office equipment was expensive.	Ausstattung
file [faɪl]	I have many files in the office.	Aktenordner
furniture ['fɜ:nɪtʃə]	My office has nice furniture.	Möbel
in front of [frʌnt]	There is a table in front of the window.	vor (räumlich)
item ['aɪtəm]	Draw the items of office furniture.	Gegenstand
keyboard ['ki:bɔ:d]	You need a keyboard to operate a computer.	Tastatur

mug [mʌg]	The pens are in the mug.	Becher
printer ['prɪntə]	We bought a new printer.	Drucker
screen [skriːn]	I like a big screen when I am working on the computer.	Bildschirm
shelf [ʃelf]	The books are on the shelf.	Regal
under ['ʌndə]	Your shoes are under the table.	unter

2

canteen [kæn'tiːn]	The food in the canteen is good and cheap.	Kantine
factory ['fæktri]	There is a car park next to the factory.	Fabrik
next door [ˌnekst 'dɔː]	She lives next door to my brother.	nebenan
opposite ['ɒpəzɪt]	There is a cinema opposite my office.	gegenüber
workplace ['wɜːkpleɪs]	Where's your workplace ?	Arbeitsplatz

3

ago [ə'gəʊ]	I was in England two years ago.	vor (zeitlich)
art [ɑːt]	He met an art student.	Kunst
building site ['bɪldɪŋ saɪt]	In 1964 Tokyo was one large building site.	Baustelle
busy ['bɪzi]	She's very busy.	beschäftigt
to carry ['kæri]	The train carries many people.	befördern
computer-controlled [kəm'pjuːtə kənˌtrəʊld]	In Japan there are computer-controlled trains.	computergesteuert
driverless ['draɪvələs]	The train is driverless.	ohne Fahrer
even ['iːvn]	There is even a beer museum.	sogar
to grow [grəʊ]	The number of pubs is growing.	wachsen, ansteigen

high-rise ['haɪraɪz]	I live in a high-rise.	Hochhaus
lion ['laɪən]	The name of the pub is 'The Lion'.	Löwe
motorway ['məʊtəweɪ]	There are speed limits on the motorway.	Autobahn
recent ['ri:snt]	Drinking tea in a pub is a recent trend.	neuer
to rediscover [ˌri:dɪ'skʌvə]	He rediscovered Tokyo after 40 years.	wiederentdecken
to taste [teɪst]	The wine tastes of apples.	schmecken
variety [və'raɪəti]	There is a large variety of shops.	Vielfalt
writer ['raɪtə]	Davies is an English writer.	Schriftsteller/-in
youth hostel ['ju:θ ˌhɒstl]	I stayed at a youth hostel.	Jugendherberge

4

air-conditioned ['eə kənˌdɪʃnd]	The conference room is air-conditioned.	klimatisiert
apartment block [ə'pɑ:tmənt ˌblɒk]	He lives in a very big apartment block.	Wohnblock
business ['bɪznɪs]	We met our business colleagues.	Geschäfts-
casual ['kæʒuəl]	It's a party; wear casual clothes.	ungezwungen, leger
date counter ['deɪt ˌkaʊntə]	This button is for the date counter.	Datumsanzeige
dial ['daɪəl]	The watch has different dials for the date and the year.	Zifferblatt
elegant ['eləgənt]	She's wearing an elegant black dress.	elegant
face [feɪs]	Your watch has a large face.	hier: Zifferblatt (Uhr)
facility [fə'sɪləti]	The hotel has many facilities.	Einrichtung
fashionable ['fæʃnəbl]	I always have fashionable clothes.	modisch
gym [dʒɪm]	There is a gym in the hotel.	Fitnessraum; Turnhalle
hand [hænd]	The hands on your watch are not going round.	Zeiger
heaven ['hevn]	It tastes like heaven.	Himmel
heavy ['hevi]	Help me! This is heavy.	schwer

to import ['ɪmpɔ:t]	He imports Swiss watches.	importieren
numerals ['nju:mərəlz]	I can't read the numerals on your watch.	Ziffern
part [pɑ:t]	A watch has hundreds of small parts.	Teil
to recommend [ˌrekə'mend]	Can you recommend a good restaurant?	empfehlen
second hand [ˌsekənd 'hænd]	Your watch doesn't have a second hand.	Sekundenzeiger
solid ['sɒlɪd]	It's a solid table.	fest
sporty ['spɔ:ti]	He's a sporty person.	sportlich
strap [stræp]	I need a new strap for my watch.	Armband
suitable ['su:təbl]	Is 6 o'clock suitable for you?	passend
syllable ['sɪləbl]	The word 'computer' has three syllables.	Silbe
traditional [trə'dɪʃnl]	Rösti is a traditional Swiss meal.	traditionell
trend [trend]	I think video phones will be the next trend.	Trend
trendy ['trendi]	She's a trendy girl.	modisch, trendig
understanding [ˌʌndə'stændɪŋ]	The symbols are for easy understanding.	Verständigung, Verstehen
winder ['waɪndə]	There's no winder on this watch - it's digital.	Aufziehschraube

5

to agree [ə'gri:]	Do you agree?	einverstanden sein, zustimmen

6

booking ['bʊkɪŋ]	I'd like to confirm my booking.	Reservierung
to confirm [kən'fɜ:m]	I confirmed my booking.	bestätigen
managing director [ˌmænədʒɪŋ dɪ'rektə]	My father is the managing director at 'Meyer's'.	Geschäftsführer/-in

7

to catch [kætʃ]	I didn't catch that.	(umgangssprachlich) mitkriegen
expression [ɪk'spreʃn]	I learnt a new expression.	Ausdruck
to follow ['fɒləʊ]	I can't follow you.	folgen
to repeat [rɪ'pi:t]	Can you repeat that?	wiederholen

Unit 5

1

bicycle ['baɪsəkl]	I go to school by bicycle / bike.	Fahrrad
jet [dʒet]	A jet is faster than a train.	Düsenflugzeug

2

airport ['ɛəpɔ:t]	Heathrow airport is very large.	Flughafen
announcement [ə'naʊnsmənt]	I listened to the announcement.	Durchsage
check-in ['tʃekɪn]	You should go to the check-in.	Abfertigung
commuter [kə'mju:tə]	A commuter travels to work every day.	Pendler/-in
to depart [dɪ'pɑ:t]	What times does the train depart?	abfahren
to drive [draɪv]	He drives very fast.	fahren
gate [geɪt]	Do you know the gate number?	Flugsteig
journey ['dʒɜ:ni]	How did you make your journey?	Reise
missing ['mɪsɪŋ]	A word is missing.	fehlen
petrol (GB) ['petrəl]	Petrol is expensive in Germany.	Benzin

platform ['plætfɔ:m]	The train leaves from platform three.	Gleis
railway ['reɪlweɪ]	The British railway system is private.	Eisenbahn
return ticket [rɪ'tɜ:n ˌtɪkɪt]	Did you get a return ticket?	Rückfahrkarte
to take off [ˌteɪk 'ɒf]	What time does the plane take off?	starten
to take [teɪk]	The journey takes two hours.	dauern

3

to build [bɪld]	They built a new hotel near the station.	bauen
carriage ['kærɪdʒ]	The train carriage was old.	Wagen
chilled ['tʃɪld]	I'd like a glass of chilled champagne.	gekühlt
to construct [kən'strʌkt]	He constructed a train.	konstruieren
cuisine [kwɪ'zi:n]	The French are famous for their cuisine.	Küche
excursion [ɪk'skɜ:ʃn]	We went on an excursion.	Ausflug, Exkursion
meadow ['medəʊ]	The train passes through meadows.	Wiese
passenger ['pæsɪndʒə]	The train was full of passengers.	Fahrgast
restaurant car ['restrɒnt kɑ:]	The restaurant car is in the middle of the train.	Speisewagen
traveller ['trævələ]	The traveller made a long journey.	Reisende/-r
via ['vaɪə]	The train goes via Paris.	über

4

timetable ['taɪmteɪbl]	Where is the timetable?	Fahrplan

5

map [mæp]	I need to buy a map of Austria.	(Land-)Karte
original [ə'rɪdʒənl]	The original route went to Istanbul.	ursprünglich
period ['pɪəriəd]	a period of 10 years	Periode
to save money [ˌseɪv 'mʌni]	I'm saving money for my holidays.	Geld sparen
strategy ['strætədʒi]	What strategies do you have to learn vocabulary?	Strategie
travel agent ['trævl ˌeɪdʒənt]	I spoke to a travel agent.	Angestellte/-r im Reisebüro
whole [həʊl]	I stayed there the whole day.	ganz

6

according to [ə'kɔːdɪŋ]	Group the words according to the instructions.	nach, gemäss
to jump [dʒʌmp]	He jumped into the pool.	springen

7

beauty parlour ['bjuːti ˌpɑːlə]	She goes to the beauty parlour once a week.	Schönheitssalon

8

to appear [ə'pɪə]	The story appeared the next day.	erscheinen
to beat [biːt]	My heart started to beat rapidly.	schlagen
to bless [bles]	God bless you!	segnen
both [bəʊθ]	I'll miss both of you.	beide
doorbell ['dɔːbel]	She rang the doorbell.	Türklingel
each [iːtʃ]	They cost £2 each.	jede/-r/-s

front page [ˌfrʌnt 'peɪdʒ]	I read the front page of the newspaper.	Vorderseite, Titelseite
to get married [ˌget 'mærɪd]	When did you get married?	heiraten
to give up [ˌgɪv 'ʌp]	I never give up easily.	aufgeben
hand-made ['hændmeɪd]	She wore a hand-made wedding dress.	hier: selbst genäht; selbst gemacht
to happen ['hæpn]	What is going to happen?	passieren
hem [hem]	She found a note in the hem.	Saum
to hope [həʊp]	I hope she will find a job.	hoffen
joy [dʒɔɪ]	You are the joy of my life.	Freude
lose [lu:z]	I will never lose hope.	verlieren
marriage ['mærɪdʒ]	They have a very happy marriage.	Ehe
mystery ['mɪstəri]	The story is called 'Mystery of Love'.	Rätsel
note [nəʊt]	I sent her a note.	Notiz
outside [aʊt'saɪd]	She waited outside.	draussen
stitch [stɪtʃ]	The dress needed a few stitches to repair it.	(Nadel-)Stich
sure [ʃʊə]	I am sure.	sicher
tear [tɪə]	There were tears in her eyes.	Träne
to try on [ˌtraɪ 'ɒn]	Did you try on the new dress?	anprobieren
witness ['wɪtnəs]	She was the witness at their wedding.	(Trau-)Zeuge

Unit 6

1

to complete [kəm'pli:t]	Complete the sentences with the correct word.	ergänzen
haircut ['heəkʌt]	I went to the hairdresser's for a haircut.	Haarschnitt

to pay compliments [peɪ 'kɒmplɪmənts]	He paid her a compliment.	Komplimente machen
to suit [su:t]	That jacket suits you.	passen

2

to brainstorm ['breɪnstɔ:m]	Brainstorm 10 words connected with 'weather'.	gemeinsam Ideen sammeln
exciting [ɪk'saɪtɪŋ]	The match ended 0-0; not very exciting.	aufregend
indoor [ˌɪn'dɔ:]	Badminton is an indoor sport.	drinnen
sociable ['səʊʃəbl]	I don't like parties. I'm not a sociable person.	gesellig
sort [sɔ:t]	What sort of car do you have?	Art
sub-heading ['sʌbhedɪŋ]	The article has four sub-headings.	Untertitel
tactical ['tæktɪkl]	Tennis is a tactical game.	taktisch
tiring ['taɪrɪŋ]	I find swimming very tiring.	ermüdend

3

to abseil ['æbseɪl]	I had agreed to abseil down.	abseilen
city run ['sɪtirʌn]	I won the city run last year.	Stadtlauf
competition [ˌkɒmpə'tɪʃn]	There is a competition at the golf club next week.	Wettbewerb
race [reɪs]	He ran in a race.	Rennen
ski jump ['ski:dʒʌmp]	Simon Ammann won the Olympic ski jump in 2002.	Ski-Springen
sports star ['spɔts stɑ:]	I think Muhammad Ali was the greatest sports star.	Sportstar
stadium ['steɪdiəm]	Basel play in the St. Jakob stadium.	Stadion
to try [traɪ]	I always try to win.	versuchen
to win [wɪn]	I'm going to win the match.	gewinnen

4

area ['eəriə]	In my area of Switzerland there are no mountains.	Gebiet
to argue ['ɑ:gju:]	My children argue all the time.	streiten
athlete ['æθli:t]	Marathon runners are wonderful athletes.	Athleten
average ['ævrɪdʒ]	The average training distance is 11km per week.	durchschnittlich
to compete [kəm'pi:t]	I would like to compete in a swimming race.	kämpfen
competitor [kəm'petɪtə]	All the competitors are very fit.	Teilnehmer
to cycle ['saɪkl]	I can't cycle up mountains!	Rad fahren
dedicated ['dedɪkeɪtɪd]	Sports stars must be dedicated.	hingebungsvoll
dedication [ˌdedɪ'keiʃn]	You need a lot of dedication to be the best.	Hingabe
diet ['daɪət]	I'm too fat. I'm going on a diet.	Diät
distance ['dɪstəns]	42km is a long distance to run.	Distanz
extremely [ɪk'stri:mli]	You must be extremely fit to do a triathlon.	äusserst
to find out about [ˌfaɪnd 'aʊt]	Where can I find out about sport clubs in my area?	herausfinden
fit [fɪt]	After two hours in the gym I feel fit and ready.	fit
hard [hɑ:d]	Swimming in the sea is very hard.	anstrengend
to hear of [hɪə]	Have you ever heard of David Beckham?	hören von
live [laɪv]	The atmosphere at a live football match is great.	live
naval commander ['neɪvl kəˌmɑ:ndə]	My grandfather was a naval commander in the war.	Fregattenkapitän
prize [praɪz]	The first prize is $1 million.	Preis
professional [prə'feʃnl]	Professional sportspeople train every day.	professionell
runners ['rʌnəz]	The runners are coming into the stadium now.	Läufer
studio ['stju:diəʊ]	In the studio today, my guest is …	Studio
successful [sək'sesfʊl]	He's a successful businessman.	erfolgreich
tough [tʌf]	The training is tough.	hart

to train [treɪn]	You need to train every day if you want to be the best.	trainieren
triathlon [traɪ'æθəlɒn]	A triathlon has swimming, running and cycling.	Triathlon
World Championships [ˌwɜːld 'tʃæmpiənʃɪps]	The World Championships are in a different country every year.	Weltmeisterschaft

5

across [ə'krɒs]	We ran across the sand.	über
cheer [tʃɪə]	They came to cheer us.	zujubeln, anfeuern
dip [dɪp]	Let's go for a quick dip.	hier: Kurzbad; kurz eintauchen
to donate money to [dəʊˌneɪt 'mʌni]	The organisers donate the money to charity.	Geld stiften, spenden
to raise money for [reɪz 'mʌni]	He raised money for charity.	Geld sammeln, aufbringen
roof [ruːf]	The house has a red roof.	Dach
sea [siː]	He swam in the sea.	Meer
to video ['vɪdiəʊ]	I videoed the film on TV last night.	auf Video aufnehmen

6

annual ['ænjuəl]	This year's annual dinner is on a Saturday night.	jährlich
developing countries [dɪ'veləpɪŋ ˌkʌntrɪz]	Developing countries need charities to help them.	Entwicklungsländer
donation [də'neiʃn]	Please give a donation to charity.	Spende
downhill course ['daʊnhɪl kɔːs]	This is a difficult downhill course.	Abfahrt
health care scheme ['helθ keə skiːm]	In Switzerland, the health care scheme is mainly private.	Gesundheitswesen
hole [həʊl]	There are 18 holes on a golf course.	Loch

maximum ['mæksɪməm]	There is a maximum of 15 people in our group.	Maximum
minimum ['mɪnɪməm]	The minimum donation is £10.	Minimum
non-stop ['nɒnˌstɒp]	The flight was non-stop to Sydney.	Nonstopp
participant [pɑː'tɪsəpənt]	There were 100 participants in the competition.	Teilnehmer
politics ['pɒlətɪks]	A lot of people don't like talking about politics.	Politik
relay race ['riːleɪ reɪs]	The 100m relay race is very exciting.	Staffellauf
to re-write [ˌriː'raɪt]	Could you please re-write your homework.	noch einmal schreiben
science ['saɪəns]	I'm not very good at science.	Wissenschaft
sponsor ['spɒnsə]	Migros is the main sponsor for this event.	Sponsor
sponsorship ['spɒnsəʃɪp]	Sponsorship is important for a football club.	finanzielle Unterstützung
tournament ['tɔːnəmənt]	There is a golf tournament in America next week.	Turnier
trophy ['trəʊfi]	The captain lifted the trophy into the air.	Trophäe

9

all-round [ˌɔːl 'raʊnd]	Swimming is good for all-round fitness.	allround, allgemein
basic ['beɪsɪk]	You can't be a good player if your basic technique is wrong.	grundlegend
body ['bɒdi]	Sport exercises your body.	Körper
breathing ['briːðɪŋ]	Yoga helps you with correct breathing.	Atmung
care [keə]	There is personal care.	Betreuung
early bird ['ɜːli bɜːd]	Are you an early bird?	Frühaufsteher
to exercise ['eksəsaɪz]	Yoga exercises your breathing.	üben
exercise ['eksəsaɪz]	Exercise is good for you.	(Gymnastik-)Übungen
fitness ['fɪtnəs]	I go to the fitness centre every Monday and Wednesday.	Fitness
flexibility [ˌfleksə'bɪləti]	Children have much better flexibility than most adults.	Beweglichkeit

to focus on ['fəʊkəs]	Today we are focusing on the 'present perfect'.	fokussieren
gentle ['dʒentl]	Yoga is a gentle sport.	sanft
to harmonise ['hɑːmənaɪz]	Yoga harmonises mind and body.	harmonisieren, ausgleichen
to increase [ɪn'kriːs]	Yoga increases your flexibility.	erhöhen
introduction [ˌɪntrə'dʌkʃn]	The first lesson was a good introduction to the course.	Einführung
link [lɪŋk]	There is a new train link from the city to the village.	Verbindung
main point [ˌmeɪn 'pɔɪnt]	The main point of fitness is to stay healthy.	Schwerpunkt
mind [maɪnd]	Yoga relaxes your mind.	Geist
needs [niːdz]	Some children have special needs in school.	Bedarf / Bedürfnisse
power ['paʊə]	Exercises in the gym will give you more power.	Kraft
to relieve [rɪ'liːv]	Yoga can relieve stress.	lindern, abbauen
resistance [rɪ'zɪstəns]	When you swim, you feel the resistance of the water.	Widerstand
routine [ruː'tiːn]	What's your training routine?	Routine
session ['seʃn]	We had a good session on the bicycles yesterday.	Sitzung (Zeitperiode)
sleepy ['sliːpi]	This brings your sleepy body to life.	schläfrig
specific ['spəsɪfɪk]	They have specific needs.	bestimmte
spinning ['spɪnɪŋ]	I go to a spinning class every week.	Rad fahren im Fitnesszentrum
stationary ['steɪʃənri]	You can ride on stationary bikes.	feststehend
stress [stres]	Stress can be positive and negative.	Stress
supervision [ˌsuːpə'viʒn]	Don't use the gym without supervision.	Aufsicht
supervisor ['suːpəvaɪzə]	Wait until the supervisior arrives before you start.	Aufseher
to support [sə'pɔːt]	The supervisor will support you.	unterstützen
technique [tek'niːk]	Your technique is good.	Technik
whatever [wɒt'evə]	You can cycle whatever the weather is like.	was/wie auch immer
workout ['wɜːkaʊt]	This is the best time for a workout.	Workout

10

balloon ride [bə'lu:nraɪd]	I want to go on a balloon ride.	Ballonfahrt
to download ['daʊnləʊd]	You can download from the Internet.	etwas runterladen
environment [ɪn'vaɪrənmənt]	You can work in a different environment.	Umgebung
incentive [ɪn'sentɪv]	Sales people need an incentive.	Anreiz, Ansporn
sales [seɪlz]	She is a sales manager.	Verkaufs-

Unit 7

1

to ask a favour ['feɪvə]	Can I ask you a favour?	um einen Gefallen bitten
to borrow ['bɒrəʊ]	Can I borrow your pen please?	ausleihen
to complain [kəm'pleɪn]	He's always complaining about the weather.	sich beschweren
to do a favour ['feɪvə]	Can you do me a favour?	einen Gefallen tun
to empty ['empti]	Can you empty my letterbox for me when I'm on holiday, please?	leeren
to give a lift [gɪv ə 'lɪft]	Can you give me a lift?	jmdn. im Auto mitnehmen
ideal [aɪ'di:l]	Can you describe your ideal neighbour?	ideal
It depends. [dɪ'penz]		Es kommt darauf an.
letterbox (GB) ['letəbɒks]	The postman puts the letters in the letterbox.	Briefkasten
lunch break ['lʌntʃbreɪk]	I sometimes go shopping in my lunch break.	Mittagspause
neighbour ['neɪbə]	We've got new neighbours.	Nachbar/-in
to switch [swɪtʃ]	Can you switch holiday dates with me?	tauschen
You're absolutely right. ['æbsəlu:tli]		Sie haben ganz Recht.

2

apart from [ə'pɑ:t frəm]	The shop is open every day apart from Sunday.	mit Ausnahme
auto parts (US) ['ɔ:təʊ pɑ:ts]	You can buy auto parts at the gas station.	Autozubehör
bakery (US) ['beɪkəri]	I get fresh bread at the bakery every morning.	Bäckerei
barber's shop (US) ['bɑ:bəz ʃɒp]	John goes to the barber's shop once a month.	Coiffeurladen für Herren
bookstore (US) ['bʊkstɔ:]	Have you been to the new bookstore?	Buchhandlung
car supplies (GB) ['kɑ: səˌplaɪz]	You can buy car supplies at the garage.	Autozubehör
chemist's (GB) ['kemɪsts]	You can buy medicine at the chemist's.	Apotheke
deli (US) ['deli]	I sometimes get my sandwiches at the deli.	Delikatessenladen
dental surgery (GB) ['dentl ˌsɜ:dʒəri]	I don't like going to the dental surgery.	Zahnarztpraxis
to do with ['du: wɪð]	I could do with a cup of tea.	gebrauchen
early-closing day [ˌɜ:li 'kləʊzɪŋ deɪ]	Wednesday is early-closing day in our village.	der Tag, an dem die Geschäfte ab Mittag geschlossen haben
exception [ɪk'sepʃn]	Wednesday is the exception - we close at lunchtime.	Ausnahme
family dentistry (US) [ˌfæməli 'dentɪstri]	I don't like going to the family dentistry.	Zahnarztpraxis
fire department (US) ['faɪə dɪˌpɑ:tmənt]	My brother works at the fire department.	Feuerwehrzentrale
fire station ['faɪə ˌsteɪʃn]	My brother works at the fire station.	Feuerwehrzentrale
to function ['fʌŋkʃn]	The post office also functions as a grocer's.	fungieren
groceries ['grəʊsərɪz]	The post office also sells groceries.	Lebensmittel
hair salon (US) ['heə ˌsælɒn]	Ann goes to the hair salon once a month.	Coiffeursalon
hairdresser's (GB) ['heədresəz]	Which hairdresser's do you go to?	Coiffeursalon
high school (US) ['haɪsku:l]	Our kids go to the local high school.	weiterführende Schule
infrastructure ['ɪnfrəstrʌktʃə]	Do you have a good infrastructure in your community?	Infrastruktur

motel [məʊ'tel]	Motels are normally cheaper than hotels.	Motel
museum [mju'zi:əm]	The little museum in Gloucester is very interesting.	Museum
phone card ['fəʊnkɑ:d]	Here, you can use my phone card.	Telefonkarte
police department (US) [pə'li:s dɪˌpɑ:tmənt]	Our community doesn't have a police department.	Polizeirevier
police station (GB) [pə'li:s ˌsteɪʃn]	Our community hasn't got a police station.	Polizeirevier
to post [pəʊst]	Could you post a letter for me?	einwerfen
public library [ˌpʌblɪk 'laɪbrəri]	Do you go to the public library very often?	öffentliche Bibliothek
public restrooms (US) [ˌpʌblɪk 'restru:mz]	Where are the nearest public restrooms?	öffentliche Toiletten
secondary school ['sekəndri sku:l]	Our children go to the local secondary school.	weiterführende Schule
services ['sɜ:vɪsɪz]	The services where we live are very good.	Dienstleistungen
to take into consideration [kənˌsɪdə'reɪʃn]	Take local facilities into consideration when you move.	in Betracht ziehen
unnecessary [ʌn'nesəsri]	Which services do you think are unnecessary?	unnötig

3

airmail ['eəmeɪl]	I'd like to send this by airmail.	(mit) Luftpost
ancient ['eɪntʃnt]	There were lots of temples in ancient Greece.	alt, historisch
character ['kærəktə]	The Russians use different characters from us.	hier: Schriftzeichen
clay [kleɪ]	The pot is made out of clay.	Ton
cloth [klɒθ]	The coat is made out of heavy cloth.	Stoff
date [deɪt]	What dates do you want to switch?	Termin
envelope ['envələʊp]	This envelope is too small for the letter.	Briefumschlag, Kuvert
to fold [fəʊld]	Fold the letter before you put it in the envelope.	falten

handwriting ['hændraɪtɪŋ]	My handwriting is very bad.	Handschrift
to invent [ɪn'vent]	When did they invent envelopes?	erfinden
material [mə'tɪəriəl]	What material is the pot made out of?	Material
papyrus [pə'paɪrəs]	Papyrus was used before paper.	Papyrus
parchment ['pɑ:tʃmənt]	Parchment was used for writing.	Pergament
printing ['prɪntɪŋ]	When printing was invented, the world changed.	(Papier-)Druck
proper ['prɒpə]	A snack is not as good as a proper meal.	richtig
tablet ['tæblət]	They used to write on tablets of clay.	hier: Täfelchen
thousands ['ðaʊzəndz]	Thousands of years ago, there was no paper.	Tausende
wood [wʊd]	You can make paper out of wood.	Holz

4

abroad [ə'brɔ:d]	Have you ever been abroad?	im Ausland
leaflet ['li:flət]	I read about the service in a leaflet.	Handzettel

Unit 8

1

diverse ['daɪvɜ:s]	Switzerland is very diverse with a lot of different regions.	unterschiedlich, verschiedenartig
multicultural [ˌmʌlti'kʌltʃrl]	A multicultural country has many cultures.	multikulturell
multilingual [ˌmʌlti'lɪŋgwəl]	Switzerland has four languages. It is multilingual.	mehrsprachig

2

aim [eɪm]	My aim is to learn English.	Ziel(-setzung)
as much (...) as possible ['pɒsəbl]	I want to learn as much English as possible.	so viel (…) wie möglich
at first [ət 'fɜ:st]	At first the children respond in English.	zuerst
bilingual [ˌbaɪ'lɪŋgwl]	My children are bilingual.	zweisprachig
by the time [baɪ ðə 'taɪm]	By the time they start school, they can read a little.	bis
external [ɪk'stɜ:nl]	The rate for external students is £15.	extern
fee [fi:]	What are your fees?	Gebühr
formal schooling [ˌfɔ:ml 'sku:lɪŋ]	Many successful businessmen did not do well during their formal schooling.	(obligatorische) Schulbildung
Just hold the line. ['həʊld ðə laɪn]		Bleiben Sie am Apparat.
nursery school ['nɜ:sri sku:l]	Most children go to nursery school when they are three.	Kindergarten
pre-school age ['pri:sku:l ˌeɪdʒ]	My children are still at pre-school age.	Vorschulalter
primary school ['praɪmri sku:l]	I started primary school at the age of five.	Grundschule
private ['praɪvət]	My children go to a private school.	privat
privileged ['prɪvəlɪdʒd]	The president's son is in a privileged position.	privilegiert
to respond [rɪ'spɒnd]	At first the children respond in English.	antworten
three-year-old ['θri:jɪəəʊld]	This is a class for three-year-olds.	Dreijährige/-r
total immersion [ˌtəʊtl ɪ'mɜ:ʃn]	Some people think that total immersion is the best way to learn a language.	Immersionsunterricht

4

accounting system [ə'kaʊntɪŋ ˌsɪstəm]	Each country has a different accounting system.	Buchhaltungssystem
at present [ət 'preznt]	At present I work in a hospital.	zur Zeit

border ['bɔːdə]	Lake Constance is on the border of Switzerland, Germany and Austria.	Grenze
broken ['brəʊkn]	My washing-machine is broken.	kaputt, ausser Betrieb
chap [tʃæp]	He's a very nice chap.	Mann (Umgangssprache)
cosmopolitan [ˌkɒzmə'pɒlɪtn]	New York is a really cosmopolitan city.	kosmopolitisch
countryside ['kʌntrɪsaɪd]	The Irish countryside is very green.	Landschaft
home town [ˌhəʊm 'taʊn]	What's your home town? – Brighton.	Heimatstadt
to improve [ɪm'pruːv]	I'd like to improve my Italian.	verbessern
to learn the trade [lɜːn ðə 'treɪd]	Jimmy wants to learn the trade from his father.	sich ausbilden lassen
outlook ['aʊtlʊk]	My grandfather has a wonderful outlook on life.	Einstellung
since [sɪns]	I've lived here since 1992.	seit

5

to apply [ə'plaɪ]	I'm going to apply for a new job.	sich bewerben
associate [ə'səʊsiːeɪt]	What do you associate with Christmas?	verbinden
BA [ˌbiː 'eɪ]	She has a BA in History.	Bachelor of Arts (ein akademischer Abschluss)
be in touch [tʌtʃ]	Sorry, I haven't been in touch.	in Verbindung sein, sich melden
container port [kən'teɪnə pɔːt]	Hong Kong is a container port.	Containerhafen
to expect [ɪk'spekt]	I expect you to win the race.	erwarten
financial centre [faɪˌnænʃl 'sentə]	The financial centre of London is called 'the City'.	Finanzzentrum
hard-working [ˌhɑːd 'wɜːkɪŋ]	The people of Hong Kong are hard-working.	fleissig
health insurance ['helθ ɪnʃʊərəns]	Health insurance is expensive.	Krankenversicherung
importance [ɪm'pɔːtəns]	What I am going to tell you is of great importance to your future.	Wichtigkeit

in writing ['raɪtɪn]	Apply in writing.	schriftlich
income tax ['ɪnkʌm tæks]	Everyone has to pay income tax.	Einkommenssteuer
Just imagine! [ˌdʒʌst ɪ'mædʒɪn]		Stell' dir vor!
native speaker [ˌneɪtɪv 'spi:kə]	My French teacher was a native speaker.	Muttersprachler/-in
Not to worry! [ˌnɒtə 'wʌri]		Keine Sorge!
of all places [əv 'ɔ:l ˌpleɪsɪz]	I met her at a football match, of all places.	ausgerechnet
sender ['sendə]	What's the sender's name and address?	Absender
starting date ['stɑ:tɪŋ deɪt]	The starting date of the new film is the 22nd October.	Anfangsdatum
Take care. [keə]	Write to me soon. Take care.	Pass auf dich auf.
well-educated [ˌwel 'edjukeɪtɪd]	The people of Hong Kong are well-educated.	gut ausgebildet
to wonder ['wʌndə]	I wonder how much that jacket costs.	sich fragen

6

atmosphere ['ætməsfɪə]	There was a good atmosphere in the school.	Atmosphäre; Umgebung
at our cost [kɒst]	We will replace it at our cost.	auf unsere Kosten
to attend [ə'tend]	I attended an important meeting in London last week.	teilnehmen
business meeting ['bɪznɪs ˌmi:tɪn]	I've got a business meeting in Prague tomorrow.	Geschäftssitzung
confirmation [ˌkɒnfə'meɪʃn]	Please send a confirmation in writing.	Bestätigung
to go wrong [ˌgəʊ 'rɒŋ]	Something has gone wrong.	schief gehen
travel agency ['trævl ˌeɪdʒənsi]	We booked the holiday through a travel agency.	Reisebüro

Unit 9

1

adventurer [əd'ventʃərə]	Charles Lindbergh was a famous adventurer.	Abenteurer/-in
backpack ['bækpæk]	My backpack is always too heavy!	Rucksack
to bleed [bli:d]	I cut my finger and it's bleeding.	bluten
branch [brɑ:ntʃ]	There is a bird sitting on the branch of that tree.	Ast
to define [dɪ'faɪn]	Can you define the word 'barber'?	definieren
definition [ˌdefə'nɪʃn]	What's the definition of 'hotelier'?	Definition
to disturb [dɪ'stɜ:b]	Please don't disturb.	stören
hike [haɪk]	I went for a hike last weekend.	Wanderung
hot-air balloon [ˌhɒteə bə'lu:n]	Bertrand Piccard travelled round the world in a hot-air balloon.	Heissluftballon
humidity [hju:'mɪdəti]	The humidity is very high in summer.	(Luft-)Feuchtigkeit
I can't be bothered. ['bɒðəd]		Ich habe keine Lust.
in my opinion [ə'pɪnjən]	In my opinion, Australia is a fascinating place.	meiner Meinung nach
inhabited [ɪn'hæbɪtɪd]	The north of Australia is inhabited by only a few people.	bewohnt
injured ['ɪndʒəd]	I injured myself when I fell down.	verletzt
lodge [lɒdʒ]	The fishing lodge is in the middle of the forest.	Hütte
mule [mju:l]	A mule is half donkey and half horse.	Maultier
path [pɑ:θ]	The path went through the forest.	Pfad
profession [prə'feʃn]	What profession are you in?	Beruf
to realise ['rɪəlaɪz]	I didn't realise what time it is.	merken
river ['rɪvə]	The Amazon is the longest river in the world.	Fluss
slope [sləʊp]	This is the best ski slope in winter.	Hang
solo ['səʊləʊ]	Charles Lindbergh flew solo across the Atlantic.	allein

to stand in for [stænd 'ɪn fə]	Could you stand in for me at the presentation?	vertreten
steep [stiːp]	The slope is very steep.	steil
straight away [ˌstreɪtə'weɪ]	I'll do it straight away.	sofort
sweaty ['sweti]	I was sweaty from the long hike in the hot sun.	verschwitzt

2

to babysit ['beɪbisɪt]	Could you babysit for us this evening?	babysitten
challenge ['tʃæləndʒ]	Learning a new language is a big challenge!	Herausforderung
check-list ['tʃeklɪst]	I have a check-list of what to do.	Liste mit Punkten, die zu prüfen sind
conference room ['kɒnfrəns ruːm]	The meeting took place in a conference room.	Konferenzraum
electronics [ˌɪlek'trɒnɪks]	She's an electronics engineer.	Elektronik
memo(randum) [ˌmemə'rændəm]	Can you send a memo to Personnel about that?	Memo, Notiz
obligation [ˌɒblɪ'geɪʃn]	Try our product with no obligation to buy.	Verpflichtung
off-licence ['ɒflaɪsəns]	Can you get a bottle of wine from the off-licence, please?	Wein- und Spirituosenhandlung
personal assistant [ˌpɜːsnl ə 'sɪstənt]	The manager has a personal assistant.	persönliche/-r Referent/-in
to rely on [rɪ'laɪ]	I know I can rely on you.	auf jmdn. zählen
request [rɪ'kwest]	Please send us your booking request.	Bitte

3

canoeing [kə'nuːɪŋ]	Canoeing is a popular sport.	Kanu fahren
chartered accountant [ˌtʃɑːtəd ə'kaʊntənt]	A chartered accountant checks the accounts.	staatlich geprüfte/-r Bilanzbuchhalter/-in
to chat [tʃæt]	We chatted for two hours on the phone.	sich unterhalten

to climb [klaɪm]	Have you ever climbed a mountain?	besteigen
climbing ['klaɪmɪŋ]	Climbing is my favourite sport.	Klettern
to come true [ˌkʌm 'tru:]	Dreams can come true.	wahr werden
to cope with [kəʊp]	I can't cope with all this work.	fertig werden mit
dream [dri:m]	Dreams can come true.	Traum
female ['fi:meɪl]	There aren't many female boxers.	weiblich
to fight [faɪt]	She tried to fight the stress.	gegen etwas ankämpfen
freelance ['fri:lɑ:ns]	I work as a freelance accountant.	freiberuflich
to hand in (your) notice ['nəʊtɪs]	I've decided to hand in my notice.	kündigen
instructor [ɪn'strʌktə]	My instructor taught me to do it better.	Lehrer/-in, Trainer/-in
less [les]	Jane now earns less money.	weniger
to make a decision [dɪ'sɪʒn]	They made the decision at the meeting.	eine Entscheidung treffen
male-dominated ['meɪl ˌdɒmɪneɪtɪd]	Most business is male-dominated.	von Männern dominiert
pleasant ['pleznt]	Jane had a very pleasant lifestyle in Jersey.	angenehm
pros and cons [ˌprəʊz n 'kɒnz]	Every job has its pros and cons.	Für und Wider
rewarding [rɪ'wɔ:dɪŋ]	They say nursing is a rewarding job.	lohnend, dankbar
satisfaction [ˌsætɪs'fækʃn]	I get no satisfaction from my job.	Zufriedenheit
stressful ['stresfʊl]	Jane's job was very stressful.	stressig
university course [ˌju:nɪ'vɜ:səti kɔ:s]	I did a university course in philosophy.	Universitätsstudiengang

Unit 10

1

to break down [breɪk 'daʊn]	My car broke down on the way to work.	kaputt gehen
to clear [klɪə]	Would you like me to clear the table?	aufräumen

dry cleaner's [ˌdraɪ 'kliːnəz]	My best jacket is at the dry cleaner's.	chemische Reinigung
excuse [ɪk'skjuːs]	I always have an excuse for not doing my homework.	Ausrede
figures ['fɪgəz]	Do you have the sales figures for 1999?	Kennzahlen
to get off [get 'ɒf]	Get off the bus at the town centre, go left ...	aussteigen
late [leɪt]	Sorry I'm late. My watch is broken.	spät

2

ad(vert) ['ædvɜːt]	Look at this ad.	Annonce
to boost [buːst]	This can boost your energy.	aufputschen
cell (cellular) phone (US) ['sel fəʊn]	Can I borrow your cell phone?	Mobiltelefon, Handy
concept ['kɒnsept]	The centre has a new fitness concept.	Konzept
to co-operate [kəʊ'ɒpəreɪt]	It's easier to co-operate than to fight all the time.	kooperieren
diary ['daɪri]	Write a diary.	Tagebuch
fear [fɪə]	I'm not going up there. I have a fear of heights.	Angst
goal planning ['gəʊl plænɪŋ]	Every winter we have a goal planning meeting.	Zielsetzung
growth [grəʊθ]	The language market has seen growth in the last 10 years.	Wachstum
hurry ['hʌri]	I'm always in a hurry.	Eile, Hektik
instant ['ɪnstənt]	He had instant success with his book.	unmittelbar
instead of [ɪn'sted əv]	Instead of sitting at home you should do some sport.	anstatt
to keep up [kiːp 'ʌp]	Life is so fast - it's difficult to keep up.	mitkommen, mithalten
to manage ['mænɪdʒ]	Do you manage your time well?	einteilen
pager ['peɪdʒə]	The doctor has a pager.	Pager
priority [praɪ'ɒrəti]	My family is my priority.	Vorrang (haben)
remote control [rɪˌməʊt kən'trəʊl]	Can you pass me the remote control, please?	Fernbedienung
to set a watch [set ə 'wɒtʃ]	I always set my watch five minutes too fast.	Uhr stellen

sickness ['sɪknəs]	Do you have 'hurry sickness'?	Krankheit
to slow down [sləʊ 'daʊn]	You should slow down; it's dangerous to drive so fast.	verlangsamen
to speed up [spi:d 'ʌp]	We need to speed up the learning process.	beschleunigen
survey ['sɜ:veɪ]	Let's do a class survey.	Überblick
terrifying ['terəfaɪɪŋ]	There were some terrifying pictures on the news.	erschreckend
unemployed [ˌʌnɪm'plɔɪd]	He is unemployed.	arbeitslos

3

advice [əd'vaɪs]	Can you give me some advice?	Rat(-schlag)
do's & don'ts [ˌdu:z n 'dəʊnts]	Here are some do's and don'ts for learning.	was man tun und nicht tun soll
optional ['ɒpʃənl]	This homework is optional.	wahlweise, freiwillig
to pick up ['pɪk ʌp]	I pick up the kids from school every day.	abholen
wedding anniversary ['wedɪŋ ˌænəˌvɜ:sri]	It's our 10th wedding anniversary next week.	Hochzeitstag

4

clothing ['kləʊðɪŋ]	I spend a lot of money on clothing for the family.	Kleidung
expenses [ɪk'spensɪz]	Don't forget your travel expenses!	Spesen
holiday entitlement ['hɒlədeɪ ɪnˌtaɪtlmənt]	How many days holiday entitlement do you have?	Urlaubstage
personnel manager [ˌpɜ:sə'nel ˌmænɪdʒə]	The personnel manager looks after the people in a company.	Personalchef/-in
regulations [ˌregju'leɪʃnz]	These are the new company regulations.	Vorschriften

to remind [rɪ'maɪnd]	Just a quick note to remind you to send me your report.	erinnern
to reply [rɪ'plaɪ]	Reply to her e-mail.	beantworten, erwidern
so far [səʊ 'fɑː]	They haven't lost a game so far this season.	bis jetzt

6

latest ['leɪtɪst]	Have you heard the latest news?	neueste/-r/-s
opportunity [ˌɒpə'tjuːnəti]	This project is a good opportunity for me.	Gelegenheit
permanent ['pɜːmənənt]	Do you have a permanent contract?	hier: fest (fester Vertrag)
promotion [prə'məʊʃn]	There are chances of promotion.	Beförderung
secure [sɪ'kjʊə]	This is a secure position.	sicher

7

although [ɔːl'ðəʊ]	Although it was raining, she went out.	obwohl
drawer ['drɔːə]	What's in your office drawer?	Schublade
herbal tea [ˌhɜːbl 'tiː]	Herbal tea is good for a bad stomach.	Kräutertee
mouldy ['məʊldi]	That sandwich is mouldy. You can't eat it!	verschimmelt
odd [ɒd]	They have odd eating habits.	komisch, seltsam
to prefer [prɪ'fɜː]	I prefer tea to coffee.	vorziehen
ready-made meals [ˌredimeɪd 'miːlz]	British supermarkets have so many ready-made meals.	Fertiggerichte
rotting ['rɒtɪŋ]	There's rotting food in the cupboard.	verfault
sell-by date ['selbaɪ deɪt]	This food is past its sell-by date.	Verfallsdatum
snack counter ['snæk ˌkaʊntə]	There's a snack counter near the front of the shop.	Regal mit Süssigkeiten, etc.
study ['stʌdi]	We are doing a study of eating habits.	Studie

unrefrigerated [ˌʌnrɪ'frɪdʒəreɪtɪd]	You shouldn't keep meat unrefrigerated for more than an hour.	ungekühlt

8

contrast ['kɒntrɑ:st]	The contrast between Europe and Africa is very big.	Unterschied
overweight [ˌəʊvə'weɪt]	He's doing fitness because he's overweight.	Übergewicht

9

can't stand [kɑ:nt 'stænd]	She can't stand the food in the canteen.	nicht ausstehen können
convenient [kən'vi:niənt]	It's convenient to have a shop near our house.	praktisch, angenehm
to dunk [dʌnk]	I love dunking chocolate biscuits in my coffee.	eintunken
to encourage [ɪn'kʌrɪdʒ]	She encourages her children to eat fresh fruit.	ermutigen
fat-free ['fætfri:]	I have fat-free milk in the morning.	fettfrei
freshly-squeezed ['freʃli ˌskwi:zd]	Freshly-squeezed orange juice is good, but expensive.	frisch gepresst
fuel ['fju:əl]	Have you put fuel in the car?	Benzin, Treibstoff
handbag ['hændbæg]	She can't go out without her handbag.	Handtasche
horrible ['hɒrəbl]	Those hamburgers look horrible.	schrecklich
low-fat ['ləʊfæt]	The supermarket has a good choice of low-fat food.	fettarm
nowadays ['naʊədeɪz]	People are more interested in healthy food nowadays.	heutzutage
on the run [rʌn]	She's on the run from morning to night.	unterwegs
pocket ['pɒkɪt]	There's a hole in my pocket.	Tasche
protein-rich ['preʊti:n rɪtʃ]	Eat protein-rich food if you want energy.	proteinreich
regular ['regjulə]	Three regular meals a day keep you healthy.	regelmässig
snacking ['snækɪŋ]	Snacking is big business nowadays.	Zwischenmahlzeiten

unbalanced diet [ʌnˌbælənst 'daɪət]	Too many snacks can mean an unbalanced diet.	unausgewogene Ernährung
unhealthy [ˌʌn'helθi]	Fatty foods are unhealthy for you.	ungesund
vanilla [və'nɪlə]	Vanilla ice-cream is my favourite.	Vanille

10

to battle ['bætl]	I'm battling against my weight at the moment.	kämpfen
bomb [bɒm]	A bomb exploded outside the church.	Bombe
comb [kəʊm]	He always has a comb in his pocket.	Kamm
knee [niː]	Footballers often have knee problems.	Knie
knowledge ['nɒlɪdʒ]	I have no knowledge of her private life.	Wissen
sparkling ['spɑːklɪŋ]	Would you like sparkling or still water?	mit Kohlensäure
thumb [θʌm]	Your thumb is the most important finger.	Daumen

Unit 11

1

account manager [ə'kaʊnt ˌmænədʒə]	If you are an important customer, you have an account manager.	Kundenbetreuer/-in
advantage [əd'vɑːntɪdʒ]	What's the advantage of this product?	Vorteil
to afford [ə'fɔːd]	I can't afford a holiday this year.	sich leisten
business trip ['bɪznɪs trɪp]	He went on a business trip.	Geschäftsreise
to commute [kə'mjuːt]	I commute between Zurich and Basel.	pendeln
disadvantage [ˌdɪsəd'vɑːntɪdʒ]	What are the disadvantages of this plan?	Nachteil
disciplined ['dɪsəplɪnd]	She is very disciplined.	diszipliniert

employer [ɪm'plɔɪə]	Migros is the biggest private employer in Switzerland.	Arbeitgeber
inefficient [ˌɪnə'fɪʃnt]	Some colleagues are inefficient.	ineffizient
isolation [ˌaɪsə'leɪʃn]	Lots of people live in isolation.	Vereinsamung, Abgeschiedenheit
personally ['pɜːsnəli]	Well, personally I think it's not OK.	persönlich
skyrocket ['skaɪrɒkɪt]	Prices skyrocketed last year.	in die Höhe schiessen
telecommuter ['telikə'mjuːtə]	A telecommuter works at home.	jmd., der/die zu Hause am Bildschirm arbeitet
time-consuming ['taɪmkənsjuːmɪŋ]	Commuting by tram is very time-consuming.	zeitaufwendig
time-saving ['taɪmseɪvɪŋ]	Telecommuting can be time-saving.	zeitsparend
traffic jam ['træfɪk dʒæm]	There are a lot of traffic jams.	Stau
uncomfortable [ʌn'kʌmftəbl]	This chair is very uncomfortable.	unbequem
unreliable [ˌʌnrɪ'laɪəbl]	The system is unreliable.	unzuverlässig

2

to connect [kə'nekt]	Are you connected to the Internet?	verbinden
to decrease [diː'kriːs]	Prices for phones have decreased.	sinken
digital camera ['dɪdʒɪtl ˌkæmrə]	I took this photo with a digital camera.	digitaler Photoapparat
integrated ['ɪntɪgreɪtɪd]	The mobile phone has an integrated camera.	integriert
to permit [pə'mɪt]	If time permits I will go to the zoo this afternoon with my family.	erlauben
to surf [sɜːf]	You can surf the Internet.	surfen
text message ['tekst ˌmesɪdʒ]	Send a text message on your mobile.	Textnachricht am Telefon (SMS)

3

electronic organiser [ˌɪlekˌtrɒnɪk 'ɔːgənaɪzə]	Do you use an electronic organiser?	elektronischer Kalender
to familiarise [fə'mɪliəraɪz]	Familiarise yourself with the Internet.	vertraut machen
fire alarm ['faɪər‿əˌlɑːm]	If the fire alarm goes off, leave the building by the stairs.	Feueralarm
intentions [ɪn'tenʃnz]	My intentions are always better than my actions!	Absichten
level ['levl]	My productivity level is better.	Niveau
own [əʊn]	I like to sleep in my own bed.	eigen
password ['pɑːswɜːd]	Don't forget your password.	Kennwort
reliable [rɪ'laɪəbl]	This system is very reliable.	zuverlässig
up-to-date [ˌʌp tə 'deɪt]	The equipment is up-to-date.	auf dem neuesten Stand

4

Best regards! [ˌbest 'rɪgɑːdz]		Viele Grüsse!
price list ['praɪs lɪst]	Could you send me a price list?	Preisliste
re [riː]	Re your enquiry = With reference to your enquiry	betreffend (in E-Mails etc.)
reference ['refrəns]	With reference to your enquiry.	Bezug

5

to disagree [ˌdɪsə'griː]	Do you disagree?	nicht einverstanden sein
prediction [prɪ'dɪkʃn]	Here are my predictions for the future.	Vorhersage
rather than ['rɑːθə θən]	They send e-mails rather than letters.	lieber als

8

to collect [kə'lekt]	I have to collect the children from school.	abholen
permission [pə'mɪʃn]	Ask for permission.	Erlaubnis
to request [rɪ'kwest]	He requested permission to leave early.	wünschen, bitten um

10

ear [ɪə]	You hear with your ears.	Ohr
eye [aɪ]	You see with your eyes.	Auge
face [feɪs]	You have a friendly face.	Gesicht
head [hed]	He put the hat on his head.	Kopf
sharp [ʃɑ:p]	The wolf has sharp teeth.	scharf
tooth, pl. teeth [tu:θ, ti:θ]	The dentist checks your teeth.	Zahn, Zähne
wolf [wʊlf]	The wolf ate the grandmother.	Wolf

Unit 12

1

awful ['ɔ:fl]	The weather was awful.	schrecklich
backache ['bækeɪk]	He gets backaches.	Rückenschmerzen
to build up ['bɪld ʌp]	You need to build up your body slowly.	aufbauen
calming ['kɑ:mɪŋ]	I find herbal tea very calming.	beruhigend
dizziness ['dɪzinəs]	Dizziness is an awful feeling.	Schwindel
dizzy ['dɪzi]	Do you sometimes feel dizzy?	schwindlig
environment [ɪn'vaɪərənmənt]	Our environment is cleaner than it was 10 years ago.	Umwelt

exhausted [ɪg'zɔ:stɪd]	I felt exhausted after the workout.	erschöpft
to let off steam [ˌlet ɒf 'sti:m]	I play squash to let off steam.	Dampf ablassen
mental ['mentl]	Golf is a very mental game.	geistig, mental
muscles ['mʌslz]	It relaxes your muscles.	Muskeln
powerful ['paʊəfʊl]	The car has a powerful motor.	kräftig
pressure ['preʃə]	She's under a lot of pressure at work.	Druck
reflexology [ˌri:flek'sɒlədʒi]	I believe reflexology can help your problem.	Reflexzonenmassage
refreshed [rɪ'freʃt]	He felt refreshed after he slept.	erfrischt
to revitalise [ˌri:'vaɪtəlaɪz]	A week's holiday can revitalise you.	wieder beleben
to rush [rʌʃ]	I had to rush to the station to catch the train.	eilen
side-effects ['saɪd ɪˌfekts]	This treatment has side-effects.	Nebenwirkungen
to switch off [swɪtʃ 'ɒf]	Sport helps me to switch off.	abschalten
tense [tens]	I often feel tense before I give a presentation.	angespannt
tension ['tenʃn]	Tension gives her headaches.	Spannung
total concentration [ˌtəʊtl ˌkɒnsən'treɪʃn]	Athletes have total concentration before a race.	totale Konzentration
tranquillity [træn'kwɪləti]	I love the tranquillity of the lake.	Ruhe und Gelassenheit
well-being [ˌwel 'bi:ɪŋ]	It's a feeling of well-being.	Wohlergehen
to work out ['wɜ:k aʊt]	Let's sit down and work out what the problem is.	herausarbeiten

2

brain [breɪn]	The brain is situated in the head.	Gehirn
to continue [kən'tɪnju:]	I'm listening. Please continue.	weiterführen, fortfahren
to postpone [pə'spəʊn]	We are postponing the meeting till next month.	verschieben

3

approach [ə'prəʊtʃ]	The new trainer has an interesting approach to diet.	Einstellung, Ansatz
balance ['bæləns]	You need a good balance of work and play.	Gleichgewicht
common ['kɒmən]	Stress is a common problem nowadays.	üblich
development [dɪ'veləpmənt]	The hotel is planning a new development.	Erweiterung, Entwicklung
feature ['fi:tʃə]	Yoga is a feature of the health programme.	Bestandteil, Element
meditation [ˌmedɪ'teɪʃn]	Meditation is something which you can do anywhere.	Meditation
mud pack ['mʌd pæk]	She looks prettier with the mud pack on!	Schlamm-Maske
nutrition [nju:'trɪʃn]	Nutrition is an important part of a healthy lifestyle.	Ernährung
to promote [prə'məʊt]	The hotel is promoting a new fitness product.	(be-)werben
rowing ['rəʊɪŋ]	Rowing is the best exercise.	Rudern
soul [səʊl]	Rest and relaxation is good for the soul.	Seele
these days ['ði:z deɪz]	We don't talk much these days.	heutzutage
to treat yourself ['tri:t jəˌself]	Why don't you treat yourself to a weekend away?	sich belohnen, sich verwöhnen
warmth [wɔ:mθ]	I love the warmth of a sauna.	Wärme

4

to meditate ['medɪteɪt]	He meditates for 20 minutes every day.	meditieren
not yet [nɒt jet]	I haven't finished the book yet.	noch nicht

5

pity ['pɪti]	It's a pity that I forgot my tennis racket. I wanted to play.	Schade, dass ...
to sail [seɪl]	Columbus sailed across the Atlantic.	segeln

6

clown [klaʊn]	The kids like the circus clowns.	Clown
funny ['fʌni]	I heard a funny joke yesterday.	lustig
illness ['ɪlnəs]	I'm afraid that this is a serious illness.	Krankheit
in good shape [gʊd 'ʃeɪp]	She's in good shape for a person of her age.	gut in Form
joke [dʒəʊk]	Tell us a joke!	Witz
to laugh [lɑ:f]	Don't laugh; it isn't funny.	lachen
laughter ['lɑ:ftə]	Laughter is the best medicine.	Gelächter, Lachen
medicine ['medsn]	Have you taken your medicine yet?	Medikament
old people's home [ˌəʊld pi:plz 'həʊm]	Her mother lives in the old people's home now.	Altersheim
patient ['peɪʃnt]	The doctor said that Jimmy was a good patient.	Patient
to recover [rɪ'kʌvə]	He recovered quickly after the accident.	sich erholen
reflex ['ri:fleks]	Let me test your reflexes.	Reflex
research [rɪ'sɜ:tʃ]	Experts are doing research in this area.	Forschung
staff [stɑ:f]	The staff at the hospital were very friendly.	Personal
therapist ['θerəpɪst]	He goes to a therapist once a week.	Therapeut
treatment ['tri:tmənt]	It's a good treatment.	Behandlung

7

age-old ['eɪdʒ əʊld]	It's an age-old practice.	uralt
common sense [ˌkɒmən 'sens]	Most advice about health is common sense.	gesunder Menschenverstand
to conflict [kən'flɪkt]	My interests conflict with my partner's interests.	widersprechen
cycle of energy [ˌsaɪkl əv 'enədʒi]	This movement creates a cycle of energy.	Energiekreis
dishwasher ['dɪʃwɒʃə]	Having a dishwasher is a great luxury for me.	Geschirrspüler

fundamental [ˌfʌndə'mentl]	The fundamental problem is that it costs too much.	grundlegend
intuition [ˌɪntju'ɪʃn]	My intuition tells me that something is wrong.	Intuition
literally ['lɪtrəli]	There were literally thousands of people at the match.	wörtlich
logical thinking [ˌlɒdʒɪkl 'θɪŋkɪŋ]	You need logical thinking for mathematics.	logische Denkweise
miserable ['mɪzrəbl]	Don't be miserable, be happy!	elend, unglücklich
to prevent [prɪ'vent]	Exercise will prevent you from becoming overweight.	verhindern
principle ['prɪnsəpl]	The basic principle of Chinese philosophy is balance.	Prinzip, Grundsatz
recommendation [ˌrekəmen'deɪʃn]	Feng Shui makes recommendations for your house.	Empfehlung
to reduce [rɪ'dju:s]	Meditation can reduce stress.	reduzieren
sink [sɪŋk]	The dirty plates are still in the sink.	Spülbecken
stove [stəʊv]	There is a saucepan of soup on the stove.	Herd, Ofen
surroundings [sə'raʊndɪŋz]	Our house is in wonderful surroundings.	Umgebung
symbolic [sɪm'bɒlɪk]	The celebration is symbolic of our victory.	symbolisch

9

mailbox ['meɪlbɒks]	Leave a message in the mailbox.	Mailbox, Briefkasten

Unit 13

1

brake [breɪk]	Don't brake so suddenly!	bremsen
bus ride ['bʌs raɪd]	Children have free bus rides.	Busfahrt
crowded ['kraʊdɪd]	The bus was crowded.	überfüllt
detective story [dɪ'tektɪv ˌstɔ:ri]	I like reading detective stories.	Kriminalgeschichte

midnight ['mɪdnaɪt]	It was midnight and very dark.	Mitternacht
novel ['nɒvl]	I prefer reading novels to other books.	Roman
pistol ['pɪstl]	The murderer shot him with a pistol.	Pistole
torch [tɔːtʃ]	I used to read at night with a torch.	Taschenlampe
wizard ['wɪzəd]	Harry Potter is a wizard.	Zauberer

2

accident ['æksɪdənt]	There was an accident on the motorway.	Unfall
basket ['bɑːskɪt]	The hot-air balloon has a large basket.	Korb
catastrophe [kə'tæstrəfi]	Climate change causes catastrophes.	Katastrophe
chain of events [tʃeɪn əv ɪ'vents]	The chain of events finished in a catastrophe.	Kette von Ereignissen
danger ['deɪndʒə]	He was in great danger.	Gefahr
day trip ['deɪ ˌtrɪp]	They went on a day trip to the mountains.	Tagesausflug
to kneel [niːl]	She was kneeling on the grass.	knien
lovely ['lʌvli]	A picnic would be lovely.	schön
to stare [steə]	The cat was staring at the birds.	starren
to steer [stɪə]	She steered the boat down the river.	steuern
suddenly ['sʌdnli]	Suddenly it began to rain.	plötzlich

3

to draw [drɔː]	It's your turn to draw a card.	(eine Karte) ziehen
to run [rʌn]	We are running a workshop.	leiten
to hitch(-hike) ['hɪtʃhaɪk]	I was hitching round New Zealand when I met her.	Autostopp machen

4

chat show ['tʃæt ʃəʊ]	I've got tickets for the chat show.	Talkshow
comedy ['kɒmədi]	I like comedy programmes.	Komödie
commercials [kə'mɜːʃlz]	He hates the commercials on TV.	Werbung
documentary [ˌdɒkju'mentri]	I saw a good documentary about Iran.	Reportage
factual ['fæktʃuəl]	I want some factual information, not opinion.	sachlich
programme ['prəʊgræm]	Which programmes do you prefer?	Sendung
viewer ['vjuːə]	Which programme has the most viewers?	Zuschauer

5

expert ['ekspɜːt]	He's an expert on Swiss history.	Experte / -in
general knowledge [ˌdʒenrl 'nɒlɪdʒ]	She has good general knowledge.	Allgemeinbildung
rehearsal [rɪ'hɜːsl]	Before the show, there was a rehearsal.	Probe
to reserve [rɪ'zɜːv]	I'd like to reserve two seats for the show.	reservieren
self-confidence [ˌself 'kɒnfɪdəns]	You need lots of self-confidence!	Selbstbewusstsein
to show [ʃəʊ]	We will show this on TV.	zeigen

6

to accept [ək'sept]	I accept your invitation!	annehmen
house-warming ['haʊswɔːmɪŋ]	Please come to my house-warming on Saturday.	Einzugsfeier

Unit 14

1

bonnet (GB) ['bɒnɪt]	Open the bonnet if you want to see the engine.	Motorhaube
boot (GB) [bu:t]	There's lots of space in the boot.	Kofferraum
headlights ['hedlaɪts]	Use your headlights in the tunnel.	Scheinwerfer
indicator ['ɪndɪkeɪtə]	The right indicator isn't working.	Blinker
mirror ['mɪrə]	Look in the mirror before you start driving.	Spiegel
petrol tank (GB) ['petrəl tæŋk]	Fill the petrol tank at the start of the journey.	Benzintank
rear light [ˌrɪə 'laɪt]	There is a problem with your rear-lights.	Rücklichter
steering wheel ['stɪərɪŋ wi:l]	Keep both hands on the steering wheel.	Lenkrad
tyre ['taɪə]	In Britain they don't have winter tyres.	Reifen
windscreen (GB) ['wɪnskri:n]	Can you see through your windscreen?	Windschutzscheibe
wing [wɪŋ]	The other car crashed into the right wing of my car.	hier: Kotflügel

2

diagram ['daɪəgræm]	They drew a diagram.	Diagramm
fascinated ['fæsɪneɪtɪd]	I'm fascinated by India.	fasziniert
guide book ['gaɪdbʊk]	They wrote a guide book for India.	(Reise-)Führer
to hitchhike ['hɪtʃhaɪk]	They hitchhiked across Europe.	Autostopp machen
lonely ['ləʊnli]	Travelling on your own can be lonely.	einsam
phrase book ['freɪzbʊk]	A phrase book helps you when you're travelling.	Sprachführer
to produce [prə'dju:s]	India produces a lot of films.	produzieren
publication [ˌpʌblɪ'keɪʃn]	The book was ready for publication.	Veröffentlichung
savings ['seɪvɪŋz]	I used my savings to buy a 'round-the-world' ticket.	Ersparnisse

trail [treɪl]	There's a nice trail through the forest.	Pfad
traveller's companion [ˌtrævləz kəm'pænjən]	This book is the best traveller's companion.	Reisebegleiter
to trek [trek]	I want to trek in Nepal.	trecken, wandern
typewriter ['taɪpraɪtə]	She wrote it on a typewriter.	Schreibmaschine
van [væn]	They drove in a van.	Lieferwagen
well-known [ˌwel'nəʊn]	Majorca is a well-known tourist resort.	bekannt
well-researched [ˌwelˌrɪ'sɜːtʃt]	The books are well-researched.	gründlich recherchiert

3

bag [bæg]	I bought two bags of shopping.	Sack, Tasche
scarf [skɑːf]	Put a scarf round your neck. It's cold!	Schal

4

accommodation [əˌkɒmə'deɪʃn]	What kind of accommodation do you offer?	Unterkunft
cottage ['kɒtɪdʒ]	We rented a cottage near the sea.	Hütte
enquire [ɪn'kwaɪə]	I'd like to enquire about a weekend break.	nachfragen
fully equipped [ˌfʊli ɪ'kwɪpt]	The kitchen is fully equipped.	gut eingerichtet
self-catering [ˌself'keɪtərɪŋ]	A self-catering apartment is good for a family holiday.	(Wohnung) mit Küche
sterling ['stɜːlɪŋ]	They take dollars, euros or sterling.	Sterling (brit. Währung)
view [vjuː]	From the mountain you can enjoy a fantastic view.	Aussicht

5

balcony ['bælkəni]	Every bedroom has a balcony.	Balkon
to cancel ['kænsl]	Don't forget to cancel your room, if you can't come.	stornieren
cancellation [ˌkænsə'leɪʃn]	Cancellation must be 7 days before.	Stornierung
check-out ['tʃekaʊt]	Check-out is before ten o'clock.	(im Hotel) sich abmelden
deposit [dɪ'pɒzɪt]	Please send us a deposit.	Anzahlung
failure ['feɪljəˌ]	Failure to cancel means loss of deposit.	Versäumnis, Nichtbeachtung
fireplace ['faɪəpleɪs]	Have you got a cottage with a fireplace?	Kamin, Cheminée
freezer ['fri:zə]	There's a freezer in the kitchen.	Tiefkühltruhe
lodge cabin [ˌlɒdʒ 'kæbɪn]	Canada has wonderful lodge cabins.	Blockhaus
loss [lɒs]	This will mean loss of your deposit.	Verlust
microwave ['maɪkrəweɪv]	The kitchen has a microwave.	Mikrowellenherd
payable ['peɪəbl]	The deposit is payable three months in advance.	zahlbar
pillow ['pɪləʊ]	Each bed has pillows.	Kopfkissen
to require [rɪ'kwaɪə]	We require written confirmation.	benötigen
utensil [ju'tensl]	They have all the cooking utensils.	Utensilien
wooden ['wʊdn]	There are lots of wooden chairs in the cabin.	hölzern, Holz-

6

to breathe [bri:ð]	Breathe the fresh mountain air!	atmen
neck [nek]	Wear a scarf round your neck.	Hals
to breathe down (my) neck [ˌbri:ð daʊn maɪ 'nek]	You're breathing down my neck.	jemandem den Platz wegnehmen, zu nahe kommen

personal space [ˌpɜːsnl ˈspeɪs]	Please respect my personal space!	hier: der Platz, den man sich in Abstand zu anderen (unbekannten) Menschen wünscht
toe [təʊ]	You're standing on my toe.	Zeh

7

to vary [ˈveəri]	The quality of his work varies from week to week.	sich unterscheiden, abweichen von
vast [vɑːst]	Canada is a vast country.	riesig, weit

8

umbrella [ʌmˈbrelə]	Take an umbrella with you; it's raining.	Regenschirm

Unit 15

to apologise [əˈpɒlədʒaɪz]	We would like to apologise for the inconvenience.	(sich) entschuldigen
apology [əˈpɒlədʒi]	Please accept my apology.	Entschuldigung
dotted line [ˌdɒtɪd ˈlaɪn]	Sign on the dotted line.	gepunktete Linie
gambling [ˈgæmblɪŋ]	You can go gambling in the casino.	spielen (um Geld)
highlight [ˈhaɪlaɪt]	Whale-watching was the highlight of my trip.	Höhepunkt
to justify [ˈdʒʌstɪfaɪ]	They justify their high prices by the high quality.	rechtfertigen
representative [ˌreprɪˈzentətɪv]	The travel company has a local representative.	Vertretung
route [ruːt]	Follow the route from Sidney to Canberra.	Route, Strecke
vineyard [ˈvɪnjɑːd]	The wine comes from a famous vineyard.	Weinberg
whale [weɪl]	The blue whale is the biggest animal in the sea.	Wal

10. Index

a, 38
a lot of, 45
Abmachungen, 26
adjectives, 47
Adjektive, 47
Adverbien, 50
adverbs, 50
  adverbs of frequency, 50
  adverbs of manner, 51
all, 46
always, 13, 50
am, 6
an, 38
any, 44
anybody, anything, etc., 41
are, 6
articles, 38
  definite, 39
  indefinite, 38
Artikel, 38
  bestimmt, 39
  unbestimmt, 38
asking the way, 63

be, 6
Befehlsform, 33
Begleiter, 34
both, 46

can, 29, 30
clock, 62
comparison of adjectives, 48
comparative form, 48
conditional, 32
continuous, 14
  present, 14, 26
  past, 19
countable, 36, 45-46
could, 29, 30
definite article, 39
determiners, 34
  articles, 38
  demonstrative adjectives, 39
  quantifiers, 44
  question words, 56
  possessive adjectives, 53
did (als Hilfsverb), 12, 17
directions, 63
Do you have ...?, 11
do/does (als Hilfsverb), 11, 14

each, 47
ever, 22
every, 13

for, 22
Fragewörter, 56
frequency, adverbs of, 50
future, 24

Gegenwartsformen, 13
going to, 27

have, 9, 11
have got, 9
have to, 31
he, 40, 41
her, 40, 41
him, 40, 41
his, 40, 41
how, 57

I, 40, 41
if, 32
imperative, 33
indefinite article, 38
indefinite pronouns, 41
infinitive, 58
-ing, 15
irregular verbs, 58
is, 6
it, 40, 41
its/it's, 43

let's, 33
lots of, 45

manner, adverbs of, 51
many, 45
may, 29, 30
me, 40, 41
Mehrzahl von Nomen, 35
Mengenangaben, 44
modal verbs, 29
Modalverben, 29
much, 45
must, 31
my, 43

needn't, 31
never, 22, 50
no, 44
nobody, nothing, etc., 42
Nomen, 34
normally, 50
nouns, 34
numbers, 62

object pronouns, 40
often, 13, 50
ordinal numbers, 62
our, 43

passive, 32
past continuous, 19

past participle, 58
past simple, 12, 16
  be, 7
  have, 12
  irregular verbs, 19
  regular verbs, 17
past tenses, 16
plural of nouns, 35
possessive 's, 44
possessives, 43
possessive determiners, 43
Präpositionen, 53
  Ort, 54
  Zeit, 53
prepositions, 53
present continuous, 14, 26
present perfect, 22
  Signalwörter, 22
present simple, 6, 9
  be, 6
  have, 9
present tenses, 13
Pronomen, 40
  Relativpronomen, 42
  unbestimmte, 41
pronouns, 40
  indefinite, 41
  relative, 42

quantifiers, 44
question words, 56

relative pronouns, 42
Relativpronomen, 42

's, 44
Satz, 56
sentences, 56
she, 41
should, 29, 31
Signalwörter, 22
  present perfect, 22
since, 22
social situations, 64
some, 44
somebody, something, etc., 42
sometimes, 50
Steigerungsformen, 48
  germanische Steigerung, 49
  romanische Steigerung, 49
  unregelmässige Formen, 49
subject pronouns, 40
Substantiv, 34
superlative form, 48

telephoning, 64
telling the way, 63
than, 48
that, 39
the, 39
their, 43
them, 41
there is / there are, 8
these, 39
they, 41
this, 39
those, 39
time, telling the, 62

unbestimmte Pronomen, 41
uncountable, 36, 45-46
unregelmässige Verben, 58
us, 41
used to, 21
usually, 50

Verben, 6
verbs, 6
verb patterns, 59
Vergangenheitsformen, 16
Vorhersagen, 25
Verlaufsform, 15

was, 7
we, 41
were, 7
what, 57
when, 56
where, 56
which, 57
  question word, 57
  relative pronoun, 42
who, 57
will, 24, 29, 31, 32
won't, 25
would, 29, 30

you, 41
your, 43

Zukunftsformen, 24